MORE PRAISE FOR

AGAINST PORNOGRAPHY

"Diana Russell's careful analysis of the causal connection between pornography and rape in *Against Pornography: The Evidence of Harm* is the most lucid and persuasive I have read. After distinguishing between pornography and erotica, Diana has reprinted standard woman-hating, vicious and violent pornographic depictions—from cartoons through to hard-core porn. Now when we speak about pornography, we all will know precisely what we are talking about. Bravo and thank you Diana Russell for your brilliant analysis, your courage and commitment."

—Jane Caputi, Ph. D., author of *The Age of Sex Crime*.

"Feminists have long tried to explain how pornography hurts women. In this book Diana Russell combines a logically compelling argument with research evidence which shows that pornography actually causes some men to rape women. But just as important: for the first time in a feminist book about pornography, she shows us the images which, she says, teach men to rape women, so the reader can see for herself what the pornography debate is all about. *Judge for yourself!*"

—Melissa Farley, Ph.D., feminist psychologist
and anti-pornography activist.

"Even in our wildest imaginations, most women are unable to fathom the vicious acts done to women by the pornography industry in the name of free speech, profit, pleasure, and yes, entertainment. Facing head-on the hatred and contempt for women exposed in visual pornography, as much as it hurts, fuels our anger and a lot of incendiary activism. After attending Diana's feminist anti-pornography slide presentation at UC-Santa Cruz one afternoon, I was moved to tear up several hundred *Hustler* magazines in convenience stores and throughout Santa Cruz."

—Nikki Craft, feminist activist against pornography and
all other forms of violence and hatred against women.

"Most women and some men think pornography is 'just sex.' They are unaware of the violence and abuse, and the dehumanisation and degradation of women in pornography, or of the bigotry and contempt and hatred of women it fosters, or of the evidence of harm experienced by women and children as a result of the use of pornography. The pornography industry thrives on this ignorance. However painful and distressing, it is essential to know the truth about pornography. Diana Russell's book shows us what we need to see and to understand in order to put an end to it."

—**Catherine Itzin, Ph.D., editor/author of** *Pornography:*
Women, Violence and Civil Liberties.

Against Pornography

Other Books by Diana E. H. Russell

Rebellion, Revolution, and Armed Force

The Politics of Rape

Crimes Against Women: The Proceedings of the International Tribunal
(with Nicole Van de Ven)

Rape in Marriage

Against Sadomasochism: A Radical Feminist Analysis
(with Robin Linden, Leigh Star, and Darlene Pagano)

Sexual Exploitation:
Rape, Child Sexual Abuse, and Workplace Harassment

The Secret Trauma: Incest in the Lives of Girls and Women

Lives of Courage: Women for a New South Africa

Femicide: The Politics of Woman Killing
(with Jill Radford)

Making Violence Sexy: Feminist Views on Pornography

Against Pornography:

THE EVIDENCE OF HARM

Diana E. H. Russell, Ph.D.

**Emerita Professor of Sociology, Mills College,
Oakland, California**

**Russell Publications
Berkeley, California**

Penthouse

For additional information, contact:
Russell Publications
2018 Shattuck #118
Berkeley, California 94704
United States of America

Cover illustration by Tim Jonke
Author photograph by Cassandra Parker
Book production by Comp-Type, Inc., Fort Bragg, CA 95437

Publisher's Cataloging in Publication
Russell, Diana E.H.
    Against pornography: the evidence of harm / by Diana E. H. Russell
    p.   cm.
    Includes index and bibliographical references.
    ISBN No. 0-9634776-1-7
    Library of Congress No. 93-092610

    1. Pornography—Social aspects. 2. Aggressiveness (Psychology).
    3. Women—Crimes against. 4. Violent crimes. I. Title.
HQ471.R87   1993   363.4'7
                                        QB193-20420

Manufactured in the United States

First Edition

WARNING

Some of the visual pornography included in this book may be distressing to some people, particularly to survivors of sexual assault.

DEDICATION

To all the feminists in the world who, in recognition of the fact that pornography is a vicious manifestation of misogyny designed to keep women subordinate to men, are committed to the fight against it.

This photo records one of many protests organized by Nikki Craft and Melissa Farley in their rampage against *Penthouse* because of the magazine's grisly photo essay on Asian women published in December 1984. An effigy of *Penthouse* owner Bob Guccione hangs over a garbage can, about to be ignited. Note the picture of Vanessa Williams (top left), for whose dethronement as Miss United States *Penthouse* was responsible, about which the rampagers were also protesting. (Photo courtesy of Melissa Farley.)

CONTENTS

PREFACE

I have come to dislike talking about the effects of pornography with people who have not seen it for themselves, or whose exposure to it has been so minimal that they equate it with pictures of nude people in sexual encounters. Many women in particular believe that they shouldn't be bothered by such pictures even though they often are. Sometimes they try to discount their dislike of many men's attachment to it with a "boys will be boys" shrug. In such circumstances, discussions on this controversial topic frequently descend into verbal combat totally removed from the reality of the degrading portrayals of women featured in these misogynist materials.

Many people are more convinced of the harmful effects of pornography after seeing visual examples of this material than by reading about the now considerable scientific evidence of harm. Many women find the visual evidence particularly convincing—*if* they look at it. But few women *do*. Others find the combination of theory and visuals particularly effective. I therefore decided to include in this book a summary of some of the scientific research on the impact of pornography together with examples of visual pornography.

Several people in the United States and abroad have told me that they found an article which I wrote on the causal relationship between pornography and rape instrumental in persuading them that pornography is dangerous to women. I decided to include this article in this book because I wanted my theory of the rape-promoting effects of pornography to be more easily available to non-academic as well as to academic readers;[1] I particularly wanted it to reach those who are working to combat pornography. I am optimistic that this book will convince many of the people

---

1   See *Political Psychology*, 9(1), 1988; Itzin, 1992; and Russell, 1993. Part of this article has been revised for my introduction to *Against Pornography*, the remainder has been revised for Part 2 of this book.

who read it with an open mind, that pornography promotes sexism, rape, and other forms of violence against women.

This book is being published just a few months after the publication of my anthology, *Making Violence Sexy: Feminist Views on Pornography*. The reason for my publishing a second book on pornography is that Teachers College Press was unwilling to take the risk of publishing the pornography pictures without my having obtained permission from the pornographers who own the copyright to them. In this, they are no different from any other publishing house. Although my essay on "Pornography as a cause of rape" is included in *Making Violence Sexy*, I feel it particularly important that the visual evidence on the harmfulness of pornography should be followed by a summary of some of the scientific evidence of harm.

I did not attempt to obtain permission from the pornographers for several reasons. I didn't want to support the pornography industry by giving them money — particularly the amount of money they would be likely to require. *Playboy*, for example, charges "$200 per cartoon for one-time North American use; $300 for worldwide use in the English language."[2] A *Hustler* representative, on the other hand, maintains that the magazine does not grant permission to reprint their materials.[3] The Photo Rights and Permissions representative at *Penthouse* refused to provide information in writing on her magazine's permissions policy, despite my efforts to obtain this, which began in October, 1992.[4] It is relevant to point out that my letters to these three magazines did not reveal my anti-pornography stance.

Another factor that would have made it impossible to even *seek* permission to reprint in some cases was my inability to trace many of the more hard-core pornography magazines whose material I wished to in-

---

2   Marcia Terrones, Rights and Permissions Administrator, Playboy Enterprises, personal communication, November 12, 1992.

3   After many phone calls to try to find out *Hustler*'s permission policy, and many cagey responses from those answering the phone, we were informed by *Hustler* representative Jeanne Diamond that, "We cannot grant permission because licensing obligations prohibit us from granting reprint rights" (November 3, 1992).

4   Letter to Maria Rothenberg, October 27, 1992; follow up letter sent February 1, 1993.

clude. Most were probably defunct by 1993, at least under the former names of their publications. It is likely that it would have been impossible to track down many of them even at the time of their publication. Probably some of them were completely underground. I was told that many such publishers deliberately avoid dating their publications. A strategy to protect themselves from prosecution for illegally using women under 18 years of age was one reason suggested for this policy.[5] Failure to date a publication also prolongs its apparent currency.

In other cases, permission was unobtainable because I no longer had any record of the sources. I have included pornographic pictures whose sources or dates I was unable to locate because this information is not needed to appreciate the degradation and abuse of women conveyed in these materials. Despite this fact, some efforts were made to document accurately the sources of the pornography included in this book. Calls to *Penthouse* proved helpful in some cases. In contrast, a *Hustler* employee maintained that it would take weeks of labor to locate the publication dates of the visuals I had faxed to her.

I have not checked the accuracy of the sources and dates of the visuals sent to me by other activists. In many cases such checking is impossible because public libraries rarely house materials which are considered pornographic, and many of the more hard-core magazines do not survive for very long. Nevertheless, I would be grateful to readers who are willing to provide any missing information and/or to correct any errors in the documentation of the visuals included here.

Another factor that influenced my decision not to seek permission to reprint pictures was that I simply could not afford the prohibitive fees that would be required in those cases where permissions might be granted. Since the only way this book could be published was to publish it myself, I had to pay all the bills that publishers normally pay. Just meeting these costs put a severe strain on my financial resources.

In addition, just because permission *can* be granted, as in the case of *Playboy,* does not mean it *will* be granted. For example, the rights and permissions administrator at *Playboy* states, "We cannot consider permission to reprint *Playboy* material in any publication until we first see a copy of the publication making the request.... If you are asking to include

---

5   Jean Barkey, personal communication to Jan Woodcock, 26 August, 1992.

our material within a book, you must first have found a publisher as *Playboy* does not grant permission to individual authors of a work."

Here is one of those proverbial Catch 22 situations. I cannot get a publisher without being able to assure them that I can obtain the appropriate permission-to-reprint documents, but, in the case of *Playboy* anyhow, I can't even *apply* for permission without already having a publisher. Were I somehow able to obtain a publisher without being able to assure them that I could get the appropriate permissions, what chance would there be of all the pornography copyright holders represented in this book giving or selling me permission rights when the book's purpose is to critique their material and point out the dangers of it to women? Pornographers invariably see feminists as their enemies. For example, this is what *Playboy* owner Hugh Hefner has been quoted as saying to his staff: "These chicks are our natural enemy.... It is time we do battle with them.... What I want is a devastating piece that takes the militant feminists apart."[6]

In short, it is safe to conclude that it would have been impossible to find a publisher for this book, even if I had sought to obtain all the reprint permissions necessary, and even had I been able to afford the high fees required for any permissions that might be granted. Since I believe that an informed evaluation of pornography requires seeing examples of the actual pictures, and that a critique without the visual evidence is far less effective, I decided to go ahead and self-publish this material. I believe that my right to free speech includes the right to publish the material necessary to show that pornography is harmful to women.

Just as smoking is not the only cause of lung cancer, so pornography is not the only cause of rape. I believe there are many factors that play a causal role in this crime.[7] I will not attempt to evaluate the relative importance of these different causal factors in this book, but merely to show the overwhelming evidence that pornography is a major one of them.

---

6   This quotation comes from a memo to staff members at *Playboy*, cited by Jacobs, 1984.
7   See Russell, 1984, for a multicausal theory of rape.

Because all viewers of pornography are not equally affected, many people conclude that pornography does not play a causative role in harm or violence toward women. This is similar to the tobacco industry's defense of cigarette smoking. They maintain that since many smokers do not die of lung cancer, smoking cannot be a cause of this disease. The mistake here is to focus on explaining individual rather than group differences; that is, the difference in the number of lung cancer cases found in smokers as a group, versus non-smokers as a group.

Similarly, instead of trying to explain why Mr. X is affected by viewing violent pornography while Mr. Y is not, we need to look at whether the average aggression scores (or whatever is being measured) of those exposed to violent pornography are significantly higher than the aggression scores of those exposed to erotica or to non-sexual, non-aggressive material.

Whereas the individual level of analysis is more relevant for clinicians, the group level of analysis is more relevant to social policy makers. Had legislators insisted on being able to understand why Mr. A kept having car accidents when he drove while drunk, but Mr. B did not, *before* they imposed stiffer penalties on drunken drivers, there would have been even more deaths on the road. Although it can be important for researchers to try to explain individual differences, we do not need this information before recognizing group effects.

This is my first experience in self-publishing, and I hope it will not be my last. Having to rely on publishers and other gatekeepers to the published word is frequently frustrating and disempowering, particularly for radical feminists. Sonia Johnson is one well-known feminist who has decided to self-publish all her books. It will be a great victory if we can find a way to bypass mainstream publishers, many of whom censor radical feminist work. Many publishers, for example, turned down my book, *Making Violence Sexy: Feminist Views on Pornography* (1993),[8] because an anti-pornography stance became unfashionable in the publishing com-

---

8   The references in the text are referred to by the last name(s) of the author(s) and the year that the work was published or, in the case of unpublished papers, presented. Complete citations for these references are at the end of the book.

munity after the Final Report of the Attorney General's Commission on Pornography was published in 1986. Neither are feminist publishers a viable alternative for scholarly work since, to my knowledge, none in the United States publish academic books by social scientists.

Distribution is probably the biggest stumbling block for self-publishers at the moment. This situation will presumably improve as increasing numbers of feminists and writers in other marginalized groups decide to bypass mainstream publishers and rely on alternative methods to get their words into print.

This self-publishing project became far more ambitious after a printing company in Oakland, California, reneged on their agreement to print the book for fear of being sued. The pornographic pictures had been repro-duced as mediocre quality halftones according to the printer's stipula-tions. In addition, the halftones were kept small so as to fit into the 5 x 8 inch page size I had chosen. At this alarming point in my publishing venture, John Fremont of Comp-Type, Inc. of Fort Bragg, California, came to the rescue. He persuaded me to obtain more professional assis-tance so that the formerly amateurish quality of the manuscript would not be used to diminish the profoundly important implications of *Against Pornography*. This required reformatting the entire manuscript, going through a lengthy editorial process, obtaining Comp-Type's assistance in distributing and marketing the book, all of which added greatly to the cost of this self-publishing effort, and delayed publication for close to a year.

Unfortunately I could not afford to get larger, higher quality halftones of the pornographic photographs made. But perhaps this fortuitous fact may serve to diminish the interest of pornography consumers in this book. Quite aside from the quality and size of the pictures included here, I anticipate that such interest would be minimal, since most pornography magazines are much cheaper than this volume and since few pornography users are likely to enjoy their masturbatory material being subjected to a critical analysis.

Roberta Harmes assisted greatly by tracking down obscure references. Several people helped with different phases of the editing process, includ-ing Mary Armour, Candida Ellis, John Fremont, Desirée Hansson, An-gela Harraway, Anna Livia, Wendy Powell, Shauna Wescott, and particularly Suzanne Popkin. Dennis Bell and Mary Anne Saunders helped with the word processing.

Jan Woodcock, Ann Simonton, Melissa Farley, and Robert Brannon generously loaned me their pornography collections from which to select photographs for this book. Jan made available to me a duplicate set of the slides and script put together by the now defunct feminist Organizing Against Pornography (OAP), as well as slides from Stopping Violence Against Women (SVAW) in Portland, Oregon, a press release on *Playboy* containing visual pornography prepared by New York-based Women Against Pornography (WAP), and a handout, also on *Playboy,* compiled by Students Organizing Against Pornography (SOAP). I am indebted to Jan for allowing me to edit and quote from her and OAP's scripts without having to go through the cumbersome practice of repeated acknowledgments. She also provided the list at the back of this book of feminist anti-pornography organizations currently active in the United States and Canada. Her contributions to this project have been invaluable.

I also had at my disposal many slides and an extensive display of visuals from pornographic magazines and newspapers which the now defunct San Francisco-based organization, Women Against Violence in Media and Pornography (WAVPM), had used, since its inception in 1976, to educate people about the harms of pornography. I am grateful to all these organizations for their contributions to this project. Many of my commentaries on visual pornography in this book have drawn on the scripts prepared by OAP, WAVPM, and other individuals and organizations. It would be far too unwieldy to acknowledge the specific sources in the section on visuals. Suffice it to say here that the commentaries about each pornographic picture represent a collaborative effort.

Several people assisted me with the metamorphosis of my original article on pornography and rape, some of which is presented in the introduction to this book, but most of which appears in Part 2. I would particularly like to thank Dorchen Leidholdt who encouraged me to publish it. She, as well as Catharine MacKinnon and Helen Longino, made some useful suggestions for revisions, and Catharine MacKinnon and Catherine Itzin were very encouraging about its value. Robert Brannon also contributed greatly to my definition of pornography and my explication of it.

I am extremely indebted to Dennis Bell, who was willing to help in whatever way I needed, applying his computer, drafting and photographic skills to the preparation of the manuscript. Without his invaluable assistance, I would not have embarked on this project on the eve of my departure from the United States. I am also exceedingly grateful to John Fremont for his role in transforming this self-publishing enterprise into one which is likely to have considerably more impact than it otherwise might have had. In addition, I am very grateful to Cynthia Frank, Mark Gatter, and Comp-Type staff members Linda Gatter and Marla Greenway who contributed their expertise and enthusiastic support to this project.

I would like to thank Suzanne Popkin and Vanessa Tait for their assistance with trans-continental communication and other vital tasks while I was in South Africa. I also anticipate that they, Dennis Bell, and Anne Mayne will help expedite the distribution of this book.

I have consulted several lawyers about the legal issues involved in publishing pornographic pictures. Of those consulted, I particularly appreciate the legal advice of Sally Kilburg, Karl Olson, Stephen Fishman, Penny Seator, Pat Grey, and legal professors Ann Scales and Catharine MacKinnon.

The encouragement I have received from many people for undertaking this project has been important to me, especially from Robert Brannon, Jane Caputi, Nikki Craft, Melissa Farley, Marny Hall, Catherine Itzin, Jeffrey Masson, Anne Mayne, Maryel Norris, Ann Scales, Ann Simonton, and Shauna Wescott.

Against Pornography:

The Evidence Of Harm

INTRODUCTION

What Is Pornography?

Proponents of the anti-pornography-equals-censorship school deliberately obfuscate any distinction between erotica and pornography, using the term erotica for all sexually explicit materials.[1] In contrast, anti-pornography feminists consider it vitally important to distinguish between pornography and erotica, and support or even advocate erotica.

Although women's bodies are the staple of adult pornography, it is important to have a gender neutral definition that encompasses gay pornography, as well as child pornography. Animals are also targets of pornographic depictions. Hence, I define *pornography* as *material that combines sex and/or the exposure of genitals with abuse or degradation in a manner that appears to endorse, condone, or encourage such behavior.*

Most of this book will focus on adult male heterosexual pornography, because most pornography is produced for this market, and because males are the predominant abusers of women. I define *heterosexual pornography* as *material created for heterosexual males that combines sex and/or the exposure of genitals with the abuse or degradation of females in a manner that appears to endorse, condone, or encourage such behavior.*

Erotica refers to *sexually suggestive or arousing material that is free of sexism, racism, and homophobia, and respectful of all the human beings and animals portrayed.* This definition takes into account that humans are not the only subject matter of erotica. For example, I remember

---

1   I have incorporated several of Robert Brannon's suggestions into my definition of pornography, as well as the definitions of the concepts within it. Personal communication, 11 March, 1992.

seeing a short award-winning erotic movie depicting the peeling of an orange. The shapes and coloring of flowers or hills can make them appear erotic. Many people find Georgia O'Keefe's paintings erotic. But erotica can also include overtly or explicitly sexual images.

The definition's requirement of non-sexism means that the following types of material qualify as pornography rather than erotica: sexually arousing images in which women are consistently shown naked while men are clothed or in which women's genitals are displayed but men's are not; or in which men are always portrayed in the initiating, dominant role. An example of sexualized racism which pervades pornography entails depictions of women that are confined to young, white bodies fitting many white men's narrow concept of beauty; i.e., very thin, large-breasted, and blonde.

Canadian psychologists Charlene Senn and Lorraine Radtke found the distinction between pornography and erotica to be significant and meaningful to female subjects in an experiment which they conducted. After slides had been categorized as violent pornography, non-violent pornography (sexist and dehumanizing), or erotica (non-sexist and non-violent), these researchers found that the violent and non-violent images had a negative effect on the mood states of their women subjects, whereas the erotic images had a positive effect (1986, pp. 15-16; also see Senn, 1993). Furthermore, the violent images had a greater negative impact than the non-violent pornographic images.[2] This shows that a conceptual distinction between pornography and erotica is both meaningful and operational.

The term *abusive* sexual behavior in my definition refers to sexual conduct that ranges from derogatory, demeaning, contemptuous, or damaging to brutal, cruel, exploitative, painful, or violent. *Degrading* sexual behavior refers to sexual conduct that is humiliating, insulting, and/or disrespectful, for example, urinating or defecating on a woman, ejaculating in her face, treating her as sexually dirty or inferior, depicting her as slavishly taking orders from men and eager to engage in whatever sex acts men want, or calling her insulting names while engaging in sex, such as bitch, cunt, nigger, whore.

Note the abuse and degradation in the portrayal of female sexuality in Helen Longino's description of typical pornographic books, magazines, and films:

---

2   These differences were significant at p <0.05 (Senn and Radtke, 1986, p. 16).

Women are represented as passive and as slavishly dependent upon men. The role of female characters is limited to the provision of sexual services to men. To the extent that women's sexual pleasure is represented at all, it is subordinated to that of men and is never an end in itself as is the sexual pleasure of men. What pleases women is the use of their bodies to satisfy male desires. While the sexual objectification of women is common to all pornography, women are the recipients of even worse treatment in violent pornography, in which women characters are killed, tortured, gang-raped, mutilated, bound, and otherwise abused, as a means of providing sexual stimulation or pleasure to the male characters (Longino, 1980, p. 42).

What is objectionable about pornography, then, is its abusive and degrading portrayal of females and female sexuality, not its sexual content or explicitness.

A particularly important feature of my definition of pornography is the requirement that *it appears to endorse, condone, or encourage abusive sexual desires or behaviors.* These attributes differentiate pornography from materials that include abusive or degrading sexual behavior for educational purposes. Movies such as *The Accused,* and *The Rape of Love,* for example, present realistic representations of rape with the apparent intention of helping viewers to understand the reprehensible nature of rape, and the agony experienced by rape victims. I have used the expression *"it appears to"* instead of *"it is intended to"* endorse, condone or encourage sexually abusive desires or behavior to avoid the difficult, if not impossible, task of establishing the intentions of pornography producers.

My definition differs from most definitions which focus instead on terms like "obscenity" and "sexually explicit materials." It also differs from the one I have used before, which limited pornography to sexually explicit materials that were abusive (Russell, 1988). I decided to avoid the concept "sexually explicit" because I could not define it to my satisfaction. In addition, I chose to embrace a long-standing feminist tradition of including in the notion of pornography all types of materials that combine sex and/or genital exposure with the abuse or degradation of women. Members of WAVPM (Women Against Violence in Pornography and Media), for example, used to refer to record covers, jokes, ads, and billboards as pornography when they were sexually degrading to women, even when nudity or displays of women's genitals were not portrayed (Lederer, 1980).

5

Some people may object that feminist definitions of pornography that go beyond sexually explicit materials differ so substantially from common usage that they make discussion between feminists and non-feminists confusing. First of all, however, there is no consensus on definitions among non-feminists or feminists. Some feminists, for example, do include the concept of sexual explicitness as a defining feature of pornography. Andrea Dworkin and Catharine MacKinnon define pornography as "the graphic sexually explicit subordination of women through pictures and/or words" (1988, p. 36). They go on to spell out nine ways in which their definition can be met, for example, "(i) women are presented dehumanized as sexual objects, things, or commodities." James Check (1985) uses the term sexually explicit materials instead of pornography, presumably in the hope of bypassing the many controversies associated with the term pornography. But these scholars have not, to my knowledge, defined what they mean by sexually explicit materials.

Sometimes there can be a good reason for feminists to employ the same definition as non-feminists. For example, in my study of the prevalence of rape, I used a very narrow, legal definition of rape because I wanted to be able to compare the rape rates obtained in my study with those obtained in government studies. Had I used a broader definition that included oral and anal penetration, for example, my study could not have been used to show how grossly flawed the methodology of the government's national surveys are in determining meaningful rape rates.

But if there is no compelling reason to use the same definition as that used by those with whom one disagrees, then it makes sense to define a phenomenon in a way that best fits feminist principles. As my objection to pornography is not that it shows nudity or different methods of sexual engagement, I see no reason to limit my definition to sexually explicit material. Unlike MacKinnon and Dworkin, who sought to formulate a definition that would be the basis for developing a new law on pornography, I have not been constrained by the requirements of law in constructing mine.

My definition of pornography does not include all of the features that commonly characterize such material, since I believe that concise definitions are preferable to complex or lengthy definitions. Pornography, for example, frequently depicts females, particularly female sexuality, inaccurately. "Pornography Tells Lies About Women" declared a bold red and black sticker designed by Women Against Violence in Pornography and Media to deface pornography. It has been shown, for example, that pornography consumers are more likely to believe that unusual sexual practices are more common than they really are (Zillmann and Bryant, 1984). These distortions often have serious consequences. Some viewers act on the assumption that the depictions are accurate, and presume that something is wrong with females who do not behave like those portrayed in pornography. This can result in verbal or physical abuse, including rape, by males who consider that they are entitled to the sexual goodies that they want or that they believe other men enjoy.

Sexual objectification is another common characteristic of pornography. It refers to *the portrayal of human beings — usually women — as depersonalized sexual things, such as "tits, cunt, and ass," not as multi-faceted human beings deserving equal rights with men.* As Susan Brownmiller so eloquently noted,

> [In pornography] our bodies are being stripped, exposed and contorted for the purpose of ridicule to bolster that "masculine esteem" which gets its kick and sense of power from viewing females as anonymous, panting playthings, adult toys, dehumanized objects to be used, abused, broken and discarded (1975, p. 394).

However, the sexual objectification of females is not confined to pornography. It is also a staple of mainstream movies, ads, record covers, songs, magazines, television, art, cartoons, literature, pin-ups, and so on, and influences the way that many males learn to see women and even children. This is why I have not included it as a defining feature of pornography.

INCONSISTENCIES IN DEFINITIONS

Many people have talked or written about the difficulty of defining pornography and erotica, declaring that "one person's erotica is another ✓ person's pornography." This statement is often used to ridicule an anti-pornography stance. The implication is that if there is no consensus on a definition of pornography, its effects cannot be examined.

Yet there is no consensus on the definitions of many phenomena. Rape is one example. Legal definitions of rape vary considerably in different states. The police often have their own definitions, which may differ from legal definitions. If a woman is raped by someone she knows, for example, the police often "unfound"[3] the case because they are sceptical about most acquaintance and date rapes. Hence, such crimes are rarely investigated. This practice certainly has no basis in the law.

If rape is defined as forced intercourse or attempts at forced intercourse, the problem of figuring out what exactly constitutes force remains. How does one measure it? What is the definition of intercourse? Does it include oral and anal intercourse, intercourse with a foreign object, or digital penetration, or is it confined only to vaginal penetration by the penis? How much penetration is necessary to qualify as intercourse? How does one determine if an attempt at rape or some lesser sexual assault has occurred? How does one deal with the fact that the rapist and even the rape survivor quite often do not believe that a rape has occurred, even when the incident matches the legal definition of rape? Many rapists, for example, do not consider that forcing intercourse on an unwilling woman qualifies as rape because they believe that a woman's "no" actually means "yes." Many women think they have not been raped when the perpetrator is their husband or lover, even though the law in most states defines such acts as rape. Fortunately, few people argue that, because rape is so difficult to define and there is no consensus on the best definition, it should therefore not be considered a heinous and illegal act.

Similarly, millions of court cases have revolved around arguments as to whether a killing constitutes murder or manslaughter.[4] No one argues that killing should not be subject to legal sanctions just because it takes a court case to decide this question.

In contrast, the often-quoted statement of one United States judge — that although he could not necessarily define pornography, he could recognize it when he saw it — is frequently cited to support the view that pornography is self-evident or entirely in the eye of the beholder. Many people have argued that because there is no consensus on how to define pornography and/or because it can be difficult to determine whether or not the pornographic label is appropriate in particular cases, pornography should therefore not be subject to legal restraint, or even opprobrium.

---

3   This is an FBI euphemism for the frequent practice by the police of discounting rape cases reported to them.

4   That a sizable proportion of the killing is womanslaughter is essentially obliterated by this term.

It is interesting to note that lack of consensus did not prove to be an obstacle in making pictorial child pornography illegal. This makes it clear that the difficulty of defining pornography is a strategy employed by its apologists in their efforts to derail their opponents by making their work appear futile.

THE CONTENT OF PORNOGRAPHY

"I've seen some soft-porn movies, which seem to have the common theme that a great many women would really like to be raped, and after being thus 'awakened to sex' will become lascivious nymphomaniacs. That...provides a sort of rationale for rape: 'they want it, and anyway, it's really doing them a favor'" — Male respondent, Hite, 1981, p. 787.

Don Smith did a content analysis of 428 "adults only" paperbacks published between 1968 and 1974. His sample was limited to books that were readily accessible to the general public in the United States, excluding paperbacks that are usually available only in so-called adult bookstores (1976). He reported the following findings:

- One-fifth of all the sex episodes involved completed rapes.

- The number of rapes increased with each year's output of newly published books.

- Of the sex episodes, 6% involved incestuous rape. The focus in the rape scenes was almost always on the victim's fear and terror, which became transformed by the rape into sexual passion. Over 97% of the rapes portrayed in these books resulted in orgasm for the victims. In three-quarters of these rapes, multiple orgasm occurred.

A few years later, Neil Malamuth and Barry Spinner undertook a content analysis to determine the amount of sexual violence in cartoons and pictorials in *Penthouse* and *Playboy* magazines from June 1973 to December 1977 (1980). They found that:

- By 1977, about 5% of the pictorials and 10% of the cartoons were sexually violent.

- Sexual violence in pictorials (but not in cartoons) increased significantly over the five-year period, "both in absolute numbers and as a percentage of the total number of pictorials."

• *Penthouse* contained over twice the percentage of sexually violent cartoons as *Playboy* (13% vs. 6%).

In another study of 1,760 covers of heterosexual magazines published between 1971 and 1980, Park Dietz and Barbara Evans reported that bondage and confinement themes were evident in 17% of them (1982).

Finally, in a more recent content analysis of videos in Vancouver, Canada, T. S. Palys found that 19% of all the scenes in a sample of 150 sexually-oriented home videos involved aggression, and 13% involved sexual aggression (1986, pp. 26-27).[5]

Of all the sexually aggressive scenes in the "adult" videos, 46% involved bondage or confinement; 23%, slapping, hitting, spanking, or pulling hair; 22%, rape; 18%, sexual harassment; 4%, sadomasochism; and 3%, sexual mutilation. In comparison, 38% of all the sexually aggressive scenes in the triple-X videos involved bondage or confinement; 33%, slapping, hitting, spanking, or pulling hair; 31%, rape; 17%, sexual harassment; 14%, sadomasochism; and 3%, sexual mutilation (1986, p. 31).

While Palys's analysis focuses largely on the unexpected finding that "adult" videos "have a significantly greater absolute number of depictions of sexual aggression per movie than triple-X videos," the more relevant point here is that violence against women in both types of pornographic videos is common, and that rape is one of the more prevalent forms of sexual violence depicted. Moreover, I would expect a comparable content analysis of videos in the United States to reveal more rape and other sexual violence than was found in this Canadian study, as the Canadian government has played a more active role than the U.S. government in trying to restrict the most abusive categories of pornography.

Palys did not find an increase in the amount of sexual violence portrayed in these videos over time. However, as he points out, it was not clear whether this was because some proprietors had become sensitized to issues of sexual violence as a result of protests by Canadian women, or

---

5   A "scene" was defined as "a thematically uninterrupted sequence of activity in a given physical context" (1986, p. 25). Only scenes involving sex, aggression, or sexual aggression were coded.

whether they hoped to avoid protests by selecting less violent fare in recent years (1986, p. 34).

In a comparison of the contents of sexual and non-sexual media violence, Malamuth (1986) points out the following important differences between them:

- While the victim is usually female in pornography, he is generally male in non-sexual portrayals of violence on television (p. 5).

- "Victims of nonsexual aggression are usually shown as outraged by their experience and intent on avoiding victimization. They, and at times the perpetrators of the aggression, suffer from the violence" (p. 6). In contrast, "when sexual violence is portrayed, there is frequently the suggestion that, despite initial resistance, the victim secretly desired the abusive treatment and eventually derived pleasure from it" (p. 6).

- Unlike non-sexual violence, pornography is designed to arouse males sexually. Such arousal "might result in subliminal conditioning and cognitive changes in the consumer by associating physical pleasure with violence. Therefore, even sexual aggression depicted negatively may have harmful effects because of the sexual arousal induced by the explicitness of the depiction" (pp. 6-7).

In summary: pornography has become increasingly violent over the years — at least in the non-video media — and it presents an extremely distorted view of rape and sexuality.

THE CIRCULATION
OF MAJOR PORNOGRAPHY MAGAZINES

The numbers of paid subscribers for selected pornography magazines are (The National Research Bureau, 1992):

Penthouse—4,600,000	*Gallery*—500,000
Playboy—3,600,000	*Oui*—395,000
Hustler—1,200,000	*Chic*—90,000

Studies conducted by many magazines indicate a pass-along readership of between two and five copies. This number is probably more like five copies for pornographic magazines because many people are embarrassed to buy their own copies, while minors may not be permitted to purchase copies by their families or by the sellers. Assuming five copies per pornographic magazine, the estimated readership of the six publications mentioned above adds up to approximately 52,000,000.

PART 1

VISUAL PORNOGRAPHY

"At last a simple cure for frigidity."
Hustler.

INTRODUCTION:

Seeing Woman-Hatred

"A picture is worth a thousand words."

Women Against Violence in Pornography and Media (WAVPM), the first feminist anti-pornography organization in the United States, was born in San Francisco in 1976 at the end of a workshop which included an extensive display of pornography. Showing women pornography remained WAVPM's major method of educating women about the relationship between pornography, sexism and violence against women. We (I was one of the founding members) gave slide presentations, exhibited pornographic pictures on large pieces of cardboard when no slide projector was available, and arranged tours of pornography stores in San Francisco. Providing opportunities for women to see pornography has become one of the basic tools of feminist anti-pornography groups throughout the United States. For example, Women Against Pornography (WAP) which was started in 1979 in New York, provided educational tours of pornography businesses in Times Square.

When I visited Denmark, the pornography capital of the world, in 1974, I bought a sample of visual pornography to take back to the United States. I wanted to show women what this so-called benign material actually looked like. (At the time, Denmark had the mistaken reputation of having reduced sexual crimes by permitting a flood of hard-core pornography to be prominently displayed all over their city.[1]) On returning

---

1   For critiques of the research that purported to show that the availability of pornography in Denmark had lowered the number of sex crimes, see, for example, Bart and Jozsa (1980) and Diamond (1980).

15

to co-teach a class on human sexuality at Mills College (an all-women's school) with three other faculty members, I showed my colleagues the material that I wanted to present to the students. I wanted the students to be able to see and judge for themselves what pornography is like, rather than having to rely on my description of it.

It is ironic that my colleagues, none of whom shared my view that such materials cause males to behave in ways that are harmful to women, refused to allow me to show it to the students. Their position was that pornography is harmless, but that it would be too distressing for students to see it! They even objected to my reading from the text that accompanied the photographs depicting the rape and torture of a woman. That was my first experience of how difficult it can be to provide women with the opportunity to look at pornography without having to go to a so-called adult sex store.

Since my colleagues first forbade me to show pornography in the class we co-taught, I have frequently organized displays of this material for my own classes there, as well as when speaking on pornography to other audiences of women. I have found that showing pornography is an effective and rapid consciousness-raiser about misogyny and male views of women. It helps to enhance women's understanding of many males' dangerous notions of what it is to be a man. It often also succeeds in arousing women viewers' anger (and some men's) at the contempt and hatred of women they see in the pictures and captions.

Women's ignorance about the true nature of pornography is not surprising. Pornography is, after all, part of male culture, like locker rooms, fraternities, football, and powerful government bodies. When women had the opportunity to see how the Senate Judiciary Committee conducted its investigation of Anita Hill's allegations of sexual harassment by Clarence Thomas, they were outraged. The assumption that men in politics make reasonable decisions and conduct themselves in a reasonable way was shattered. Instead, women saw how unable the male senators were to transcend their self-serving biases and deal fairly with one of their own whose credibility was challenged by a "mere woman."

For these reasons, I want to provide as many women as I can reach with the opportunity to see some of the portrayals of women and sex that turn males on in this and other male-dominated societies. While a self-published book can hardly satisfy my aspirations to reach millions of women, it is the best I can do at this time.

Some might think it inconsistent for anyone who believes as I do — that viewing pornography is frequently harmful to the viewer and/or their intimates — to show pornography. But the effects of seeing pornography are different when such material is presented within an anti-pornography framework. The reader may recall that I have defined heterosexual pornography as "material created for heterosexual males that combines sex and/or the exposure of genitals with the abuse or degradation of females in a manner that appears to *endorse, condone,* or *encourage* such behavior." Clearly, I am not endorsing, condoning, or encouraging pornography in this book. I am exposing and criticizing it.

Psychologists James Check and Neil Malamuth have provided experimental evidence that pornography that is supplemented with sound educational information does not induce the negative effects that would otherwise occur (1984). On the contrary, their findings reveal that pornography shown in an educational context provides the viewer with a better understanding of the material. Before this experiment was conducted, anti-pornography feminists had arrived at the same conclusion by relying initially on our intuition, and later on our experience.

Although my causal theory focuses specifically on rape, I have also selected pornography that portrays other forms of violence against women. I think it is a mistake to discount the commonality in these different manifestations of male violence. Beatings frequently accompany rape. Some rape victims are murdered. Sexual harassment sometimes involves rape. And the torture of women frequently has a sexual dimension. I have included non-violent depictions as well in order to demonstrate the misogyny in non-violent pornography.

The section on visual pornography begins with cartoons from pornographic publications. Many readers may find cartoons less disturbing than the photographs of real women that follow. Some may question my inclusion of cartoons as examples of pornography, but those I have included do meet my definition. Cartoons in pornographic magazines are also effective indicators of the owners' or producers' attitudes to women and sexual assault. Consider the *Penthouse* cartoon that is the frontispiece of this book, for example. It is inconceivable that the magazine's owner, Bob Guccione, would permit the inclusion of such a cartoon in his magazine if he considered rape to be an abhorrent act.

Many people fool themselves that the women they see in the pages of pornography are happy to be doing this kind of work; that the rapes, beatings and other forms of torture portrayed are only simulated; that the women in bondage are never hurt or humiliated while posing for the camera and never sexually assaulted before they are released from their bonds; and/or that the women have chosen to do this work so issues of harm are irrelevant, just as they are for some other dangerous occupations. But even were these views accurate, this would be no reason to discount the harm caused by the misogynist messages conveyed by these materials. Because cartoons do not involve live women, the issues of choice and harm to the women used in pornography cannot distract viewers from seeing the woman-hating messages in the cartoons.

On the other hand, those who are not targeted in the cartoons often say, "But they are only jokes! Where's your sense of humor?" as if humor wipes out the harmful effects of sexist jokes. Of course, this argument cannot be applied to pornography that uses real live women, although *Hustler* magazine frequently uses humor in these circumstances as well. I am suggesting, then, that some readers will be more disturbed by the cartoons and others by the degrading portrayals of real women. Those who discount both may have a tougher time discrediting the data and theoretical arguments presented in Part 2.

Most people probably do not consider pictures on record covers to be pornographic, but again, the two examples I include in the following pages meet my definition. Just because an image or a story is considered mainstream does not mean that it's not pornography. Many people today mistakenly believe that *Playboy* and *Penthouse* are not pornographic magazines because looking at them has become so widely accepted. The fact that millions of males use the pictures as ejaculatory material tends to be forgotten — at least, by women.[2]

Written materials are a significant part of the pornography market. Many racks of inexpensive paperback novels on a wide range of pornographic themes are a staple product in many pornography stores. The covers of some of these books, as well as a few excerpts, are included in the visual material which follows.

---

2   Of course, there is nothing wrong with sexual excitement or sexual gratification *per se*. But there *is* a serious problem when these sensations are stimulated by abusive images, including the objectification of women. This point will be addressed in greater depth in Part 2.

I have included many examples of pornography that portray contempt and/or hostility toward women without actually depicting violence. My theory about the causal relationship between pornography and rape developed in Part 2 shows how such sentiments contribute to the undermining of some males' inhibitions against acting out their desire to rape women.

For the most part, I have deliberately omitted child pornography. (I say, "for the most part," because there is no way of knowing whether some of the women photographed are minors; that is, under 18 years of age.)[3] Often when child pornography and adult pornography are addressed together, people overlook the abuse of adult women.[4]

Readers may notice that many of the examples of visual pornography were published in the 1970s. Given that the primary goal of this book is to show the causal relationship between pornography and harm, the publication date of the material isn't important. Similarly, some readers may question my inclusion of five pictures from Denmark and two from Japan. Once again, *where* pornography is published is irrelevant to whether or not it is causally related to rape and other forms of violence against women.

There are probably some otherwise sceptical readers who are willing to concede that the few examples of foreign pornography included in this book are harmful to women since they are more degrading than pornography made in the United States. Yet, aside from the fact that there is an international trade in pornography, as a result of which foreign materials are readily available in the United States, to grant that *some* pornography has a harmful effect is significantly different from arguing that all pornography is harmless. The question would then shift to *which* materials are harmful and which are not. This would be a very different public debate than the one going on over the past few years, which still questions whether any pornography is harmful.

Because of racist notions that equate female beauty with whiteness or lightness, the features of women of color who appear in pornography

---

3   Also, I have included three examples from a *Penthouse* sequence portraying females who appear to be adolescent girls (see numbers 102-104).

4   I plan to self-publish a book in the future on child pornography that will also combine theory and visual examples.

often resemble Caucasians. A careful review of the visuals will reveal a larger representation of women and men of color than a cursory examination might suggest.[5] However, I was unable to find suitable examples of pornography portraying Latina women. Whether or not this is because there is less acceptance of pornography in Catholic than in Protestant cultures is a matter for future research to determine.

Some readers may be disturbed to find themselves becoming sexually aroused by some pornographic pictures in this book despite their awareness, perhaps even abhorrence, of the misogyny they reveal. This may engender feelings of self-criticism, or even self-hatred, or it may cause these readers to feel that something is wrong with them. There are many ways in which men and women have learned to sexualize male domination and female subordination in Western societies, including being turned on by both subtle and blatant forms of female degradation. After all, we live in a male-dominated society so we should not be surprised that most males, and even some females, feel aroused by pornographic materials that celebrate sexism and woman abuse.[6]

While I think getting turned on to pornography *does* signify that our culture has made some destructive inroads into a person's psyche, as is similarly signified by discovering racist attitudes in oneself, this is no reason to embrace either pornography or racism. Rather, it indicates the importance of fighting against these phenomena for both personal and political reasons.

However, there *is* reason for great concern when those who feel aroused by pornography (or racism) become advocates or defenders of it. Many unhealthy practices are promoted in all societies, such as the consumption of unnutritional foods, cigarette smoking, alcohol consumption, spending beyond one's means. That such practices are — like pornography — encouraged in Western cultures is no reason to accept them as harmless, or to take a laissez faire attitude to them. Rather, the more destructive they are found to be, the more strenuously they should be resisted, on both personal and public levels. This book provides evidence

---

5   For a more detailed analysis of pornography and racism, see Mayall and Russell, 1993.

6   We cannot even begin to know what sexuality would be like in a truly egalitarian society. This also applies to lesbian relationships.

20

to show that pornography qualifies as deserving the most strenuous opposition we can muster.

Questions I have found useful to keep in mind when evaluating the harm that results from pornographic pictures are these:

1. Does it appear that any harm was done to the people and/or animals photographed? If not, can one be certain that no harm occurred to them in connection with their being photographed? How does the treatment appear to have differed for the males and females photographed?

2. Regardless of the fate of the participants in the pornographic pictures, what are the messages conveyed to viewers? How dangerous, traumatic, humiliating, painful or unpleasant is the treatment of the people depicted? Are males and females portrayed differently? If so, why?

It is difficult, of course, to be confident about the accuracy of one's evaluations in light of the often feigned pleasure on participants' faces. Let us never forget the numerous rapes and torture behind the smiles of Linda Lovelace (Lovelace, 1981 and 1986) in the blockbuster pornographic movie, "Deep Throat."

PORNOGRAPHIC VISUALS

1. Chic, September 1977.

Comment 1. It is easy to discount the degradation and humiliation of women evident in this cartoon because we are apt to discount such negative intentions when they are cloaked in humor. But consider what it means to equate women with dogs in an anthropomorphic culture. Note that the word "bitch" is a derogatory term for women; that this "bitch" is portrayed as smiling and happy with her fate; that she so identifies with being a bitch, that she wags her behind to greet the approaching dog; that her nonchalant, hip-looking master appears to have forgotten that he has a woman at the end of his chain — naked, except for her black sadomasochistic collar, halter and boots — in contrast with the dog owner who seems a bit startled at this sight; and last, but not least, that she is being taken to obedience school. I saw a woman treated in very similar fashion to the "bitch" here on a KQED[7] TV-documentary on sadomasochism except that her master was taking her on a leash to the local supermarket in Ukiah, California.

---

7   KQED is the prestigious educational television station in California.

Comment 2. This cartoon reinforces the stereotype of women as stupid — they can't tell their ass from their elbow. The woman's nudity here is totally gratuitous.

2. Penthouse, September 1984.

Comment 3. This cartoon reinforces dangerous, racist stereotypes about African American men as violent criminals and rapists.

3. *"I come home after a hard night of robbery, rape, and murder, and she gives me a light beer! Have you ever tasted light beer?!"*

Hustler, March 1981.

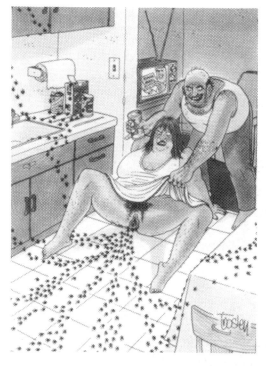

4. *"See that? It's free, and it works just as good as those expensive roach traps."*
Hustler, June 1985.

Comment 4. The TV in the background is advertising "Roach Motel" cockroach killer. Many cartoons in pornography portray women's genitals as disgusting and smelly, particularly women who do not fit pornographers' narrow notions of attractive female sex objects.

Comment 5. Jokes about sexual harassment in the work place are very common in *Playboy* and *Penthouse*, as well as in other pornography magazines. Sometimes the women are shown as willing, sometimes as distressed, and some- times, as in this cartoon, as totally neutral.

5. *"I've just been through a brutal board meeting, Ms. Kentworth. At times like this I need solace, compassion, understanding, and the usual blow job."*

Source unknown.

6. "And now, Miss Simmons, let's check the old reflexes."

Penthouse, August 1980.

Comment 6. This cartoon trivializes the problem of gynecologists sexually abusing their women patients. The insertion of an electrical plug into his patient's vagina minimizes rape by a foreign object. The cartoonist's choice of a plug implies that the gynecologist plans to turn her on. It is easy to imagine what the gynecologist will do when she has become sexually aroused.

Comment 7. The victim of sexual harassment in this cartoon is shown as totally unaffected by having to service her boss' sexual desires. This is one of many male myths surrounding sexual harassment.

7. *"Gentlemen. We here at Creative Efficiency Associates believe in the optimum use of structured time and personnel."*   *Playboy, January 1987.*

Comment 8. Here the victim is at least shown asking a question. But the artist has made it ambiguous as to whether she is more upset on realizing that her boss may withhold her monetary bonus or

8. *"You mean this is the year end Christmas bonus?"*
    Playboy.

because he is subjecting her to sexual intercourse during the office Christmas party.

9. *"You want equality? Next time we'll do it on your desk."*

Playboy, February 1979.

Comment 9. In this cartoon the harassing boss misunderstands his victim's attempt to reject him sexually. Many males share this man's difficulty in understanding women's feelings about both harassment and the meaning of equality.

10. "Remember that Christmas bonus I promised you, Miss Pettingale?"

Penthouse, December 1984

Comment 10. Here a sexual harasser is portrayed as beckoning his colleagues to come into the room to have sex with his female employee after he has finished. Her consent is irrelevant. Indeed, her Christmas bonus will be a "gang bang," suggesting that servicing these men sexually will be a positive experience for her. A used woman can be passed along to other men without her consent. She is in such a degraded and powerless position that any desire for privacy she might have is of no concern to these men; this is an occasion for men to show their sexual prowess, not to be concerned about the feelings of a lowly secretary.

11. *"You may have been more deserving of the promotion Simpson, but we felt that Wrightson had a greater need for the office."*

Playboy.

Comment 11. In this cartoon one employee is rewarded for flaunting his sexually exploitive behavior by being promoted over a more deserving colleague. In addition to conveying the management's approval of such behavior, it suggests his/their inability to distinguish between office sex and sexual harassment on the job. Not surprisingly, there is no mention of the female employee being rewarded with a private office.

12. "Relax, Miss Goodbody — you can't stop an idea whose time has
    come."   *Playboy, October 1973* .

Comment 12. Here, the woman is depicted as alarmed by her employer's sexual advances. Readers are supposed to find it funny that he intends to have sex with her anyhow, and that he thinks it is reasonable to request that she should relax in these circumstances. This is reminiscent of the well-known insult, "If you're going to be raped, you might as well lie back and enjoy it." Another subtext is that it is understandable that the woman's body and dress would "provoke" such behavior; she's *asking* to be raped.

13. "Before you go, would you mind tightening my ankles a little?"

Playboy, October 1977.

Comment 13. This cartoon reinforces the myth that women enjoy pain.

14. *"Well...at last the airlines have come up with something fresh!"*
Playboy, November 1973.

Comment 14. Here the horrifying experience of gang rape is minimized by the casual use of the slang term "gang bang," at the same time that it is normalized by the travel agency and the male speaker in the cartoon — who assumes against all reason that his female companion shares his enthusiasm.

Comment 15. This cartoon reinforces one of the most insidious of male myths: that women enjoy being raped. This notion is also one of the most popular scenarios in pornography.

15. Hustler, February 1983/4, p. 38.

16. *"The trouble with rapists is that they're never around when you need them."*

Hustler, December 1990.

Comment 16. Here is another example of the myth that women enjoy being raped. By targeting women joggers, this cartoon mocks the notion that women are out jogging to keep fit. This is particularly disturbing in light of all the women who have been raped, kidnapped, and killed when out jogging.

Comment 17. Many people do not realize that intercourse with a woman who is unable to consent because she is in some way physically helpless, constitutes rape in many states in the USA. This means that a woman who wakes up to find herself being penetrated is a victim of rape. Many men, however, believe that they are entitled to have intercourse with a sexual partner, particularly

17. "I'm sorry, I didn't mean to wake you."
Playboy.

a wife, when she is asleep. The man in this cartoon apologizes for waking the woman, not for raping her.

18. "Comfy?"   *Playboy, December 1975.*

Comment 18. This cartoon perpetuates the idea that women enjoy bondage. When women are tied up they lose whatever meagre power they have to prevent abuse in heterosexual sexual situations, which, of course, is why many males enjoy the fantasy or the practice of tying women up.

*19. "Well, I'm a consenting adult and Charley here is a consenting
adult—that makes two out of three."*   Playboy, April 1973.

Comment 19. This cartoon is not about women liking to be raped, since the about-to-be raped woman has already said no and is depicted in a defensive mode. It is about males feeling entitled to rape. Unfortunately, this sense of male entitlement is widespread.

Comment 20. Here is a visual "joke" in which train workers stop a train, not to rescue but to rape a helpless woman. In reality, some men do rape women caught in vulnerable situations. Some men, for example, pose as good Samaritans by offering to help women stranded in broken down cars, but then proceed to rape them.

20. Playboy, September 1971.

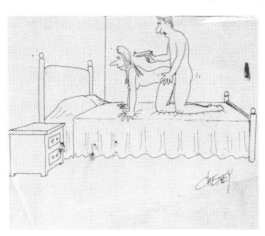

21. "You don't have to worry about getting pregnant... I've taken every precaution."   *Penthouse, May 1983.*

Comment 21. Is the rapist's intention to kill his victim the precaution that he has taken to prevent her becoming pregnant? Or is it the incongruity of a rapist bothering to reassure his victim that she won't become pregnant, while holding a gun to her head, that is supposed to be funny here? If the first interpretation is correct, it reflects the widespread assumption that rapists are exceptionally callous monsters, thus denying that many supposedly considerate and well-adjusted men rape women, and that an even larger percentage of men would *like* to rape a woman. With regard to the second interpretation, there are many instances of rapists becoming quite solicitous of their victims after the rape, giving them money for transport, or offering them coffee.

Comment 22. This picture is one of a series entitled, "Uses for Women." The text accompanying the picture reads, "Since time began women have complained, 'You're just using me for sex!' Don't get the impression that *Hustler* magazine thinks of women only as sex objects. Women can be used for many other things." The example in this first of two pictures demonstrates a woman's vagina being used as "a handy bottle opener." Another picture shows a woman being used as a serving tray for bean dip. This kind of extreme contempt for women is one of the hallmarks of *Hustler* magazine. Mocking feminist goals is another.

22. *Hustler.*

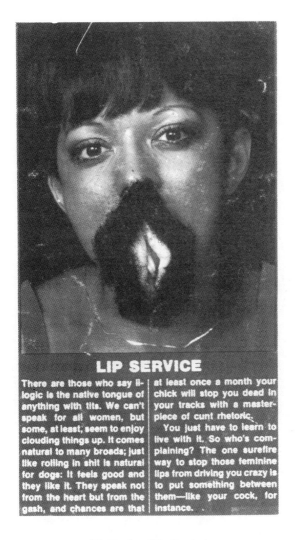

23. Hustler. (Lip Service)

Comment 23. Here is another example of *Hustler*'s blatant and lewd contempt for women.

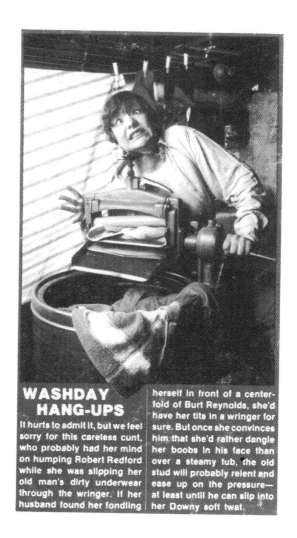

WASHDAY HANG-UPS

It hurts to admit it, but we feel sorry for this careless cunt, who probably had her mind on humping Robert Redford while she was slipping her old man's dirty underwear through the wringer. If her husband found her fondling herself in front of a centerfold of Burt Reynolds, she'd have her tits in a wringer for sure. But once she convinces him that she'd rather dangle her boobs in his face than over a steamy tub, the old stud will probably relent and ease up on the pressure— at least until he can slip into her Downy soft twat.

24. Hustler, October 1976. Wash day Hangups

Comment 24. And another.

25. *Hustler, February 1991. Nasal Sex*

Comment 25. This picture portrays women as sexual slaves whose role it is to service males' sexual needs with a smile, no matter how much pain and indignity it entails. That penetration of a nasal passage would be devoid of sexual pleasure for women illuminates how irrelevant women's real sexual desires and needs are to pornographers whose goal is to excite the sexual fantasies of their male customers.

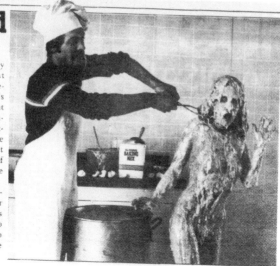

26. *Hustler, March 1981. Battered Wives*

Comment 26. This picture totally trivializes woman-beating as well as revealing *Hustler*'s contempt for women.

27. Source unknown. WAVPM display.

Comment 27. This picture illustrates a popular male fantasy that the bigger the penis the better, no matter how much pain it causes women. If the picture showed a man penetrating a woman's entire body with a weapon, it would probably amuse fewer males. But if it's a penis that does the damage, it's considered amusing.

28. Hard Boss.

Comment 28. This is the cover of a so-called "adults only" publication which sexualizes the boss/secretary relationship. On the inside cover of the magazine the secretary says, "I was in love with my boss. I wanted so badly for him to fuck me that my pussy ached with desire whenever he came within ten feet of me." She then initiates their sexual encounter. This depiction of sex in the office is a male fantasy which seriously distorts the widespread sexual harassment of secretaries by their bosses.

"Give her your best shot—and the stupid bitch will never complain again!"

29. ?Bitches Who Like it Rough[8], vol. 1, no. 1.

---

8   A question mark at the beginning of a source indicates my uncertainty that it is correct.

Comment 29. The notion that complaining women will be silenced by "a good fuck" is part of the male mythology reflected, as well as reinforced, in this cartoon. Actually the combination of sex and contempt portrayed here is antithetical to the kind of sex and caring most women desire. Note the equation of good sex with man's "best shot," and the assurance that this will stop the woman from ever complaining again. The covert message is that his best shot will stop her "bitching" or perhaps even kill her.

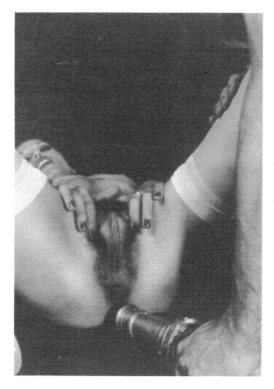

Comment 30. This photograph is the last in a series entitled "Fireman's Ball." It is preceded by several scenes of intercourse and oral sex between a fireman and the woman he is rescuing. The picture portrays the woman as so insatiable that she eagerly awaits the insertion of a fire hose nozzle into her vagina, reinforcing the idea that women like to be raped with foreign objects.

30. Swank, March 1984.

❖

The next 16 photographs provide examples of racist pornography. This is an identifiable genre in pornography that has been ignored by most progressives, including some feminists. Because women are the victims and because sex is involved, this pernicious material is trivialized as about sex rather than about eroticizing sexist racism. The element of sex makes it *more*, not *less*, dangerous.

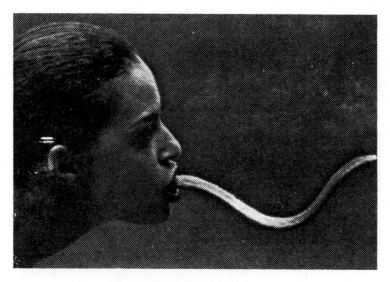

31. "They say women are all vipers."
Playboy.

Comment 31. A viper is a snake, and when people are referred to as vipers, the epithet has treacherous or venomous connotations. Despite the fact that the caption refers to all women, the picture is of an African American woman. This reinforces a sexist and racist myth that associates evil with blackness and womanhood. It also exemplifies the fact that pornography often portrays African American women as animals.

Comment 32. In *Animal Sex Among Black Women*, the author claims that African American women have a particular propensity for sex with animals. "When I began to exhaustively research the topic of the black female," he writes, in an attempt to establish scientific credentials where none exist, "I discovered that a lot of them, caught up in the escapist syndrome...had taken to having sex with animals." This pornographer's pretence that *Animal Sex* is a serious, research-based book, despite the pornographic language on every page, reinforces the racist views held by many readers of texts like this who do not realize that these "studies" are fraudulent.

ANIMAL JOURNALS

ANIMAL SEX AMONG BLACK WOMEN

by Spencer Washington

32. American Art Enterprises, Inc.,

I'LL NEVER FORGET THE NIGHT MY FATHER CAME INTO MY ROOM AND FORCED ME TO DO THOSE TERRIBLE THINGS TO HIM!

"That night, when I ran away after he slapped me, he came after me. He tied me, stripped me and raped me, telling me I'd better get to love it, telling me I'd better get used to it."

... From a tape recorded interview.

Compiled and edited for reading ease by Evette Holms.

PRINTED IN U.S.A.

33. Star Distributors, New York, 1981.

Dr. Lamb Library $2.95

ABUSE:
BLACK & BATTERED

CASE STUDIES

Comment 33. Abuse: Black and Battered purports to be one in a series of case study-based books in "Dr. Lamb's Library." The following quote, described as "from a tape-recorded interview," appears in small print on the back cover: "That night, when I ran away after he slapped me, he came after me. He tied me, stripped me and raped me, telling me I'd better get to love it, telling me I'd better get used to it."

The pornographic language, the absence of a named author, the "Adults Only" label, and the admission inside the book that "All characters in this book are fictional...," clarify the fact that the stories are a sham. Nevertheless, the feigned authenticity appears to be designed for readers who get off on "true accounts."

The book opens in the following racist fashion: "There is a myth about life in the ghetto, and the resulting attitudes about the sexual relationships between ghetto people. The myth says that all sex is abusive sex, but behind every myth, there is some truth."

34. Star Distributors, New York, 1981.

Comment 34. The racist misogyny reflected on the back cover of *Soul Slave*, by an author using the name Rita Cochran, is even more grotesque inside. For example: "Rance [a white man] looked down at me and said, 'Get naked, Nigger!' And those words were like the greatest poetry in the world to me.... It was like that man had dug down there in the deepest part of me and found something that was ultimate nigger, ultimate bitch, ultimate pain-loving whore."

" 'I am going to give you the fucking of your worthless, nigger life,' he said.... Then he cleared his throat and spit at me. A glob of spittle landed on one of my big, nigger tits.... I had never felt more alive in my life, my worthless, nigger life.... One of them [white boys] told me that I was a special nigger, that I could take more cock into my pussy than any dozen Southern belles. I thought about that and it gave me pride. There was little else that I could be proud of."

How can people who are concerned about racism continue to ignore such material?

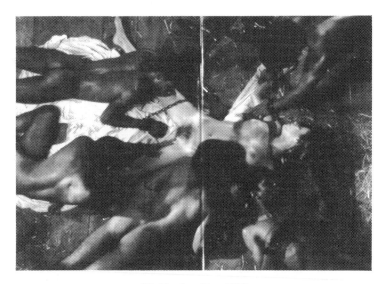

35. Hustler, May 1978.

Comment 35. This depiction of the gang rape of a white woman by African American men serves to illustrate a story entitled "Belle of the Ball." In this story, a white woman sexually entices African American men while visiting their slave quarters. The woman becomes the men's shackled slave. This story reverses the historical reality of white men invading the slave quarters and raping African American women.

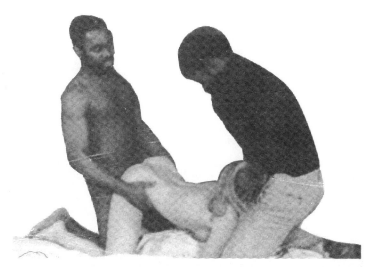

*36. "Rape fans will get off on black revolutionaries feeding their white
captive at both ends in Hot Summer."*
Source unknown. WAVPM display.

Comment 36. The term "rape fans" validates males' rape desires as if they
are acceptable, harmless, and perhaps even manly pursuits. This picture
portrays one of the most common racist stereotypes about African American males in white American culture: that African American males are
particularly prone to raping white women. The reference to black revolutionaries in particular may be intended to suggest that these men are
motivated to seek change in US society in order to have access to white
women.

Comment 37. The stories in these three paperback books sexualize atrocities during the Nazi era. Pornography with Nazi themes is an identifiable genre in US pornography. Both *Hitler's Sex Doctor* and *Expose!* advertise at the bottom of their covers that there are "ten pages of ads from people who want to meet you." Eroticizing anti-Semitism was one of the strategies used by Hitler to foster sufficient hatred toward Jews that millions of Germans would end up participating in his mass extermination campaign.

37. Publishers unknown.

Comment 38. *Sluts of the S.S.* — one book in a series called "War Horrors" — describes the repeated rape and torture of a Jewish woman by a Nazi who orders her, " 'On your knees, Jewish dog....' "

" 'You will learn to obey the Master Race....' "

" 'You will suck the dick of the master.... Open your Jewish mouth.' "

38. Star Distributors, New York, 1979.

And, " 'Whore,' he yelled. 'You will love the cock of your master.' "
The Jewish "heroine" ends up with a young Nazi as her lover.

39. Oui Magazine.

Comment 39. It is gruesome to think that a pornographer would endeavour to turn males on with a picture of a Hitler look-alike slapping a woman's bare behind. Eroticizing a genocidal dictator whose macho desire to conquer the world culminated in World War II, mocks the millions of victims, survivors, and sufferers of this agonizing historical period.

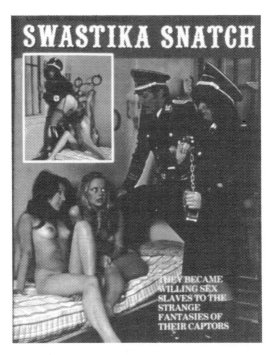

40. Swastika Snatch, vol. 1, no. 1.

Comment 40. Female sexual slavery is a common theme in pornography. In contrast to other kinds of slavery, victims of female sexual slavery are often portrayed in pornography as willing, even eager, to be enslaved. The cover provides an example of this grotesque male fantasy.

41. Hustler, vol. 7, no. 9, 1981.

Comment 41. "Fuck dolls" are frequently advertised in pornographic literature. Available by mail order or in porn stores, this "Little China Doll" reveals common racist stereotypes about Asian women as extremely submissive and knowledgeable about how to serve and "please a man."

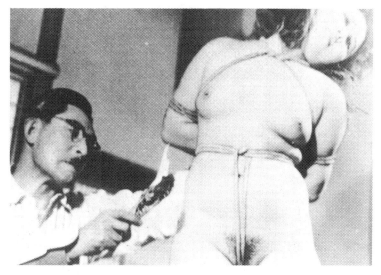

42. *Cherry Blossom, No. 3, March 1977. Utopia Publishing Co. Los Angeles.*

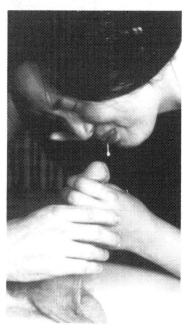

Comment 42. Asian women are a favorite target of bondage and torture in pornographic magazines. This photograph portrays a man about to burn a woman in bondage.

Comment 43. It is rare that pornographers publish such obvious expressions of disgust on women's faces. Most males prefer to believe that women become sexually excited by the sight of their sexual anatomy, and that they enjoy whatever sex acts males care to inflict on them.

43 Oriental Pussy.

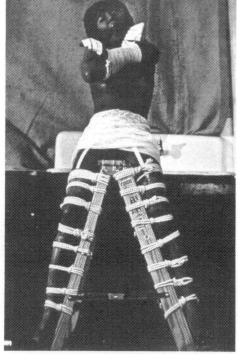

44. Source unknown.   *45. Source unknown. WAVPM slide.*

Comment 44. This picture is one of a series that focuses on the bondage of this Asian woman. The text that accompanies this picture reads, "He had made no bones about the fact that he had a fetish for Orientals. She found that disgusting, but she was interested in his obvious excitement. It was the first time since she arrived in this strange land that any man had paid attention." By the end of the series the woman is portrayed as an even more accommodating victim: "It was ugly and sordid, but...it was his pleasure to do this, and if she could accept that, she could share his pleasure. She vowed to have fun."

Comment 45. This photo comes from a magazine on Asian women in bondage. Note that this woman's genitals are inaccessible. There is considerable bondage and torture pornography that caters to males who become aroused by the idea of dominating, humiliating, and/or brutalizing women without the depiction of genital sexual contact.

46. Custer's Revenge
Video game produced by American Multiple Industries.

Comment 46. This is the cover of an X-rated video game manufactured for home use. This game entails male figures with erections moving through a maze and scoring points by raping a Native American woman. The player scoring the most rapes wins the game. This is one of the few video games that has aroused considerable protest.

Comment 47. The first sentence of the text for this photo reads: "Our moving target also spent four years exploring most of Europe." Referring to a woman and/or her vagina as "our moving target" is depersonalizing, proprietary, and an invitation to attack.

47. Penthouse, December 1985.

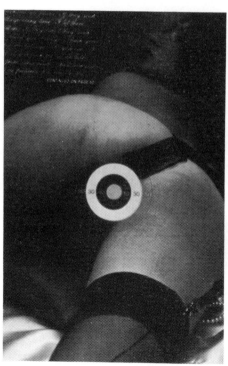

Comment 48. The woman in this picture is portrayed as *wanting* her vagina to be a target: "Think you can hit the bulls eye?" she asks. "If you can, I might let you fuck me till we both drop from exhaustion." One of WAVPM's favorite slogans was, "Pornography tells lies about women." The women invented by males to turn them on have little in common with real women.

48. ?Gallery, 1984.

Comment 49. Despite the fact that the woman in this photograph is wearing bullets around her waist, she is portrayed as vulnerable rather than threatening. Note that the bullets, which are phallic symbols, are pointing toward her vagina. Associating bullets with the body of a beautiful, aroused naked woman eroticizes them, and by extension, guns and violence.

49. Playboy, January 1985.

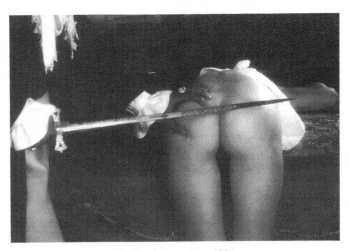

50. Penthouse, June 1986.

Comment 50. In this photograph a fully dressed man in the costume of a 17th century "gentleman" holds a sword to a woman's bare behind as if about to beat her with it. Women in pornography are often naked while the men are partially or fully clothed, as in this picture. Once again, this photo eroticizes sexual violence against women.

51. Stag.

Comment 51. The unlikely words that are put into the mouth of the woman in this picture are: "Now shove that thing in me [a gun] and fuck my pussy with it until I come all over the tip." Since what is happening in pornography influences what happens in real life, we should not be surprised to learn that some males do shove weapons up women's vaginas. Portraying women as wanting this is untrue and dangerous, as is eroticizing weapons by associating them with women and sex.

Note also that the man's gaze in this picture is on the gun, not the woman, despite the fact that he is engaged in sexual contact with her. Once again, it is the implied violence, not the sex, that captivates him. What kind of man does this appeal to? Surely not males who love women or who prefer sex to violence.

52. "Love and Kisses."

Comment 52. The association of the words "love" and "kisses" on this record cover album with the violent way in which the woman's T-shirt is being ripped and in which hands continue to grab at her, exemplifies the merging of sex and violence which is so rampant in pornography.

LET'S FACE IT, GUYS, SOME WOMEN ARE JUST BEGGING FOR ROUGH TREATMENT. THEY WHINE, THEY NAG, THEY SASS YOU BACK WHEN YOU GIVE THEM AN ORDER. THERE'S JUST ONE THING TO DO—GIVE THEM WHAT THEY DESERVE!

Comment 53. The caption to this photograph goes beyond giving men permission to beat and rape women; it positively advocates violence against women while at the same time placing the responsibility for this on women: "some women are just begging for rough treatment."

53. Take That, Bitch! vol. 1, no. 1, Eros Publishing Company, Wilmington, Delaware, 1983.

Comment 54. This photo portrays an angry man biting a woman's bottom. It condones the sexualization of aggression and the acting out of it on women's bodies. Anything males want to do to women is acceptable in pornography.

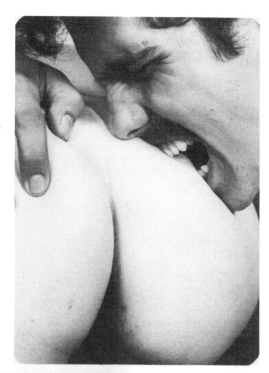

54. ?Take That, Bitch! vol. 1, no. 1, 1983.

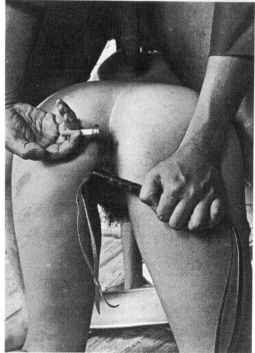

55. Cherry Blossom, No. 3, March 1977.

Comment 55. "Cherry Blossoms" connote Asian women in pornography, perhaps because of the association of cherry blossoms with Japan, the fact that the word "cherry" symbolizes innocence and virginity and that flowers are associated with women. Many women have been burned with cigarettes in the course of sex torture by men in pornographic enactments as well as in everyday life.

56. Hustler, ?1981.

Comment 56. This picture is the last in a series called "Dream Lover." At the beginning of the series, the woman is brutally beaten by her "dream man." The text reads, "She senses the erotic nature of the humiliation which he subjects her to." After being dragged by her hair to the bathroom, the woman's dream lover experience culminates in the scene shown here in which she gasps for air after her lover has forcibly submerged her head in the water of a toilet. By titling such torture as "dream lover," *Hustler* once again reinforces the notion that women are turned on by torture.

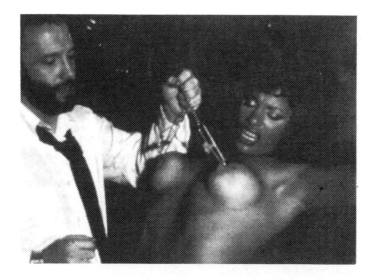

57. Hustler.

Comment 57. In this photograph titled "Rating Guide," a man is placing clamps on an African American woman's nipple. This photograph appears to be a clip from a pornographic movie called "Girls USA." When rating this movie, *Hustler*'s film critic evaluated this movie according to the stiffness of the erection it could be expected to produce. He rated the effectiveness of this film as "3/4 erect: Worthwhile. Almost gets it up. But it can still be beat." He rejected the option, "Erection: A constant turn on. If this won't get it up, you may be dead." Most males feel entitled to rate women's bodies on a routine basis, as well as to inform them about what parts they particularly like, or, when more blatantly hostile, what parts they particularly dislike. These males are bewildered by the growing recognition that such verbal behavior, including apparently complimentary assessments, constitutes sexual harassment.

*58. Un-
known
source.*

Comment 58. Long needles are being stuck into a woman's breasts in this line drawing, and a safety pin appears to have been thrust through her left nipple. The rope around her upper right arm makes it clear that she is in bondage. The pain resulting from the needle torture is very evident in her face.

*59. Cherry Blossom, No. 3,
March 1977.*

Comment 59. The pornographer who orchestrated this photograph chose a woman as the torturer. It is quite a common practice for pornographers to have women doing men's dirty work. Even though the scenario is staged, the physical pain for the woman whose genitals and surrounding areas are being pinched with clothespins must be real. Remember, it usually requires extended periods of posing to obtain publishable photographs. Once again, the pornographer responsible for this picture has eroticized hurting a woman.

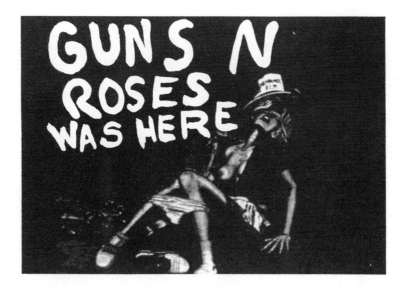

60. Guns and Roses.

Comment 60. The announcement on a record cover that "GUNS N ROSES WAS HERE," next to a raped woman, sounds like a boast by the Guns and Roses musicians that they were responsible for raping her. One wonders how many women were raped as a result of this blatant example of locker-room machismo.

Comment 61. The pornographer's idea here is to turn males on to the sight of a man on the point of cutting a woman's breast with scissors. The depiction of four hip-looking male participants (the long hair and beads) lends legitimacy to the torture portrayed and implies that this behavior is the "in" thing to do.

61. Source unknown.

62. Take That, Bitch! vol. 1, no. 1, 1983.

Comment 62. This is the cover of a glossy pornography magazine that boasts, "Over 150 Photos of Bitches Getting Belted!!!" The blurb on the lower right of the cover is equally appalling: "Orgasms Gush as Babes Bare Bottoms are Beaten!" The ridiculousness of this pornographic alliteration notwithstanding, the producer of this magazine makes it grotesquely clear that the aim of pornographers is to provide masturbation material for males — whatever it takes.

Comment 63. This picture is one in a sequence titled "Dirty Pool." It was published about two months before the highly publicized gang rape of a woman in a bar in New Bedford, Massachusetts, where she went to buy cigarettes. The rape was applauded by many male onlookers. The first picture in the series depicts a waitress being pinched by a lecherous male pool player. In the picture shown here, she appears to be turned on, lifting her breasts with her own hands to better stimulate the penis of one of her rapists. The text

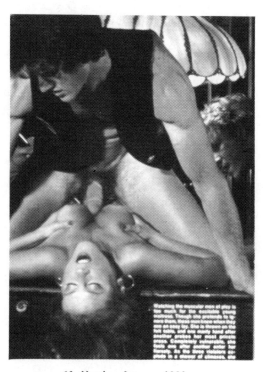

63. Hustler, January 1983.

reads: "Watching the muscular young men at play is too much for the excitable young waitress. Though she pretends to ignore them, these men know when they see an easy lay. She is thrown on the felt table, and one manly hand after another probes her private areas. Completely vulnerable, she feels one after another enter her fiercely. As the three violators explode in a shower of climaxes, she comes to a shuddering orgasm...." This portrayal of an initially reluctant woman becoming turned on and orgasmic when raped (indeed, having a simultaneous orgasm!), is one of the most popular scenarios in pornography.

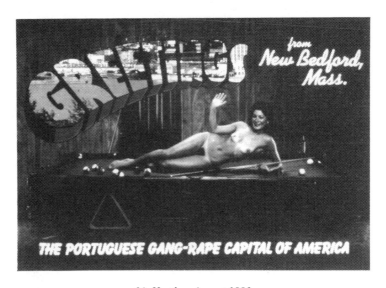

64. Hustler, August 1983.

Comment 64. This postcard was published after the New Bedford pool table gang rape. Along with insulting the rape survivor and Portuguese people, *Hustler* trivializes a rape for which owner Larry Flynt could arguably be held partially responsible.

Comment 65. Many pornographers (Hugh Hefner, Larry Flynt, and Bob Guccione, for example) appear to hate feminists and feminism with a passion. The pure viciousness of this vengeful attack on Gloria Steinem shows that Al Goldstein, the publisher of *Screw* magazine, must be included among them. The text in the upper right hand corner of the picture on the following page reads: "Unable to menstruate after years of taking male hormones, Gloria is forced to bleed for her cause by the jagged teeth of the women she taught to hate." The women portrayed as biting Gloria's genitals are covered with blood — a far more shocking sight in the original full-page color picture than here.

65. *Screw magazine, late 1970s.*

Larry Flynt also subjected Steinem to his misogynist venom by publishing a photograph of Steinem on a "Most Wanted" poster in *Hustler*, because she had urged people to engage in actions against pornography. In the course of his diatribe, Flynt claimed that she "should be considered armed with false propaganda and dangerous to the rights of all Americans." In reality, *Flynt* is the one who is armed with false propaganda, and is a menace to the rights, and lives, of all women. In this poster, Flynt has the gall to maintain that pornography is "the healthy depiction of

adult sexuality." The photographs published in this book show how removed the material from *Hustler* and other pornographic publications are
from portrayals of healthy adult sexuality. Flynt also publishes material
that legitimizes and sexualizes the sexual abuse of children, particularly
girls.

66. *Master Mandrake,
c/o ?.A.G.E. (first letter of acro-
nym missing), P.O. Box 26560,
Los Angeles, CA 90026.*

Comment 66. Excerpts from this article on *The Cinch* read as follows:
"As any experienced practitioner knows, a wrapping of rope is much
easier to escape from than a wrapping which has been cinched.... If your
object is in motion when the wrapping is being done, it may be quite
difficult to cinch your knots. The cinches may be added after the main
tying has been completed. This will ensure inescapable bondage as the
photos on this page illustrate.... Next issue: A nonfiction photo essay on
GAGS."

67. Penthouse, June 1977.

Comment 67. This picture is the first of a series in a photo essay entitled "Bound for Glory" in which abduction, bondage, and imminent rape and murder are depicted as titillating, glamorous, fashionable, and upper class. The text reads:

"Once upon a time a successful seduction occurred only after a long candlelit dinner.... No longer! Today's man wants his satisfaction, and he wants it now! Today's woman, however, still has romantic notions in her pretty little head, feminism notwithstanding. She still expects her cigarettes and her inner fires lighted. Fortunately there is a solution to this dilemma—Bondage. Simply tie her up!"

68. Bondage Love.

Comment 68. While the title of this magazine combines the concepts of love and bondage, there is no sign of love in the blurb on the cover. It is blatantly contemptuous of women, referring to so-called cock teasers as "cunts," and implying that such women should be tied up and raped if they refuse to have sex.

69. Ad in Playboy, August 1975.

Comment 69. This ad for *Oui* magazine condones incestuous abuse. In the guise of how one family solved its discipline problem, the ad announces the availability of a series of pictures of a nude adolescent girl in handcuffs on a bed. The text of the ad reads: "Lately, Jane has been very, very naughty. That's why, in the current issue of *Oui* magazine, Jane is pictured in a variety of poses that restrict her movement.... So you see, it's for her own good. And not incidentally, your pleasure." The picture in the ad guarantees that Jane will appear in *Oui* in suggestive nude poses, thereby eroticizing incestuous bondage masquerading as parental discipline.

Comment 70. This woman's pubic hair has been removed, and the chain attached to her labia is wound around her hand from the nails of which blood is dripping. This photo gives the impression that the bondage paraphernalia on the woman's body are merely decorative when, in reality, such gear is used to torture women. By eroticizing the woman's torture apparel and portraying her as enjoying pain (she uses her nails to wound herself), *Hustler* condones the torture of women.

70. *Hustler, March 1984.*

71. *Simone Devon, No. 2, August 1990. Published quarterly by London Enterprises, Van Nuys, California.*

Comment 71. This magazine presents itself as "celebrating the psychological power of the bound beauty whose love bondage is as much for her pleasure as ours." The settings in elegant homes, lawns and gardens convey an image of "gracious living" geared to reach upwardly mobile, "respectable" men. The bound woman, Stefanie, is described as the "attractive star" of "the most strikingly visual bondage videos we've ever seen!" According to the text, Stefanie "masterminded the video herself, planning the picturesque settings, imaginative lighting, and the strict bondage positions as an expression of her own personal vision of sensual restraint." Portraying women as responsible for their own victimization is commonplace in pornography.

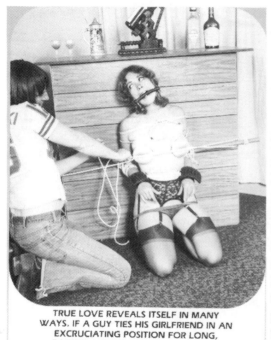

TRUE LOVE REVEALS ITSELF IN MANY WAYS. IF A GUY TIES HIS GIRLFRIEND IN AN EXCRUCIATING POSITION FOR LONG, PAINFUL HOURS, IT SHOWS HE CARES ENOUGH TO WANT HER TO BE A BETTER PERSON FOR THE EXPERIENCE. MOST GIRLS APPRECIATE THIS ATTENTION!

Comment 72. The message here is that true heterosexual love can best be expressed by a man hurting the woman he loves. The more pain he can inflict on her, the more love he shows. Note the fact that the man in the picture is fully clothed and that the tight binding of the woman's breasts is not a fantasy: a real woman had to pose like that for as long as it took to get this photograph, assuming that her exploitation by the pornographers didn't continue thereafter.

72. *?Take That, Bitch! vol. 1, no. 1, 1983.*

73. Penthouse, August 1983

Comment 73. The woman in this photograph is depersonalized by covering her entire face with what looks like black plastic. Note the large phallic object on the left of the photo which appears to have been especially constructed for this picture. This picture is part of a series entitled "Darkness at Noon." In most of the series, the woman is photographed in various states of bondage. The text includes a few quotations from the sadistic, femicidal[9] pornographic classic, *The Story of O.* For example: "First make sure to brand me with your mark...let the whole world know I am yours. As long as I am beaten and ravished on your behalf, I am naught but the thought of you, the desire of you, the obsession of you. That, I believe, is what you wanted. Well, I love you and that is what I want too."

Despite the deviousness of hiding behind arty quotations from a classic in which the woman character embraces being tortured, *Penthouse* owner Bob Guccione here gives his blessing to such torture of women for the entertainment of men. Indeed, this pictorial-cum-text sexualizes such torture and makes it appear that at least some women desire it.

---

9   The term "femicide" refers to the misogynist killing of women by men (see Radford and Russell, 1992).

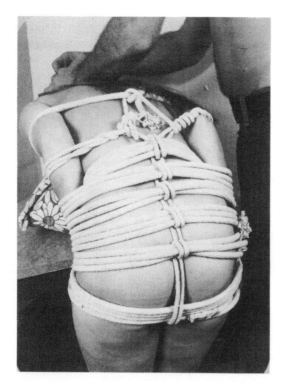

74. Source unknown.

Comment 74. The marks of the rope on the woman's buttocks are quite visible in the original of this photograph. For those who see nudity in this context as benign, why is it only the woman who is naked?

75. Kane Photo Exchange, No. 8, 1988. Published in Providence, Rhode Island.

Comment 75. The publisher of this magazine states that it accepts "amateur photos, non-fictional texts, props, and devices" from its readers. Also included are order forms for other magazines such as "Spanked Employees," "Foot Worship," and "Wet Letter" — an enema magazine showing women whose "thirsty behinds crave soapy quarts...spreading wide in anticipation." There is no attempt to glamorize the women in these pictures. The focus is on the bondage equipment, and how effectively it can enhance men's control over women.

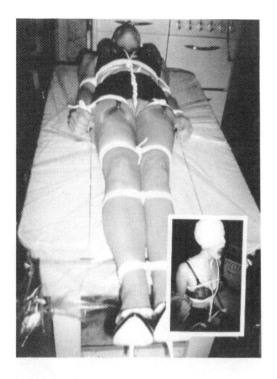

76. Kane Photo Exchange, No. 8, 1988. Published in Providence, Rhode Island.

Comment 76. This woman is totally immobilized. Clearly, any woman who is bound in this fashion, whether it occurs in the course of her work or her private life, whether she consented to it or not, is at the complete mercy of the photographer who is free to take advantage of the power and opportunity such situations offer. Negative consequences to males who exploit women in this situation are improbable since women who are violated while in bondage are unlikely to report such abuses to the police.

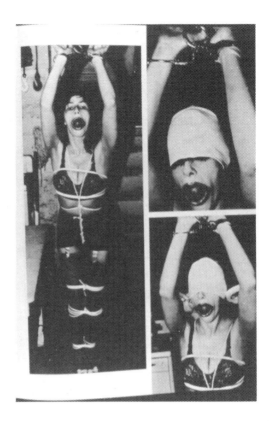

77. Kane Photo Exchange, No. 8, 1988. Published in Providence, Rhode Island.

Comment 77. These three pictures show the popular bondage ball gag which totally silences the victim. The picture on the lower right shows a head cover that obliterates the woman's vision. Note the meat hook hanging in the top left of the picture.

78. Kane Photo Exchange, No. 8, 1988. Published in Providence, Rhode Island.

Comment 78. In the lower right picture the woman is completely packaged and bound, unable to see or talk but still able to hear her master.

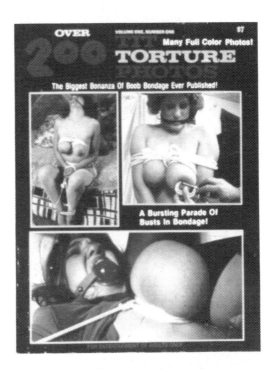

79. Tit Torture Photos, vol. 1, no. 1.

Comment 79. The subtitle on the cover of this magazine reads, "The Biggest Bonanza of Boob Bondage Ever Published!" Breast torture is a distinct genre in pornography. The notion that a woman's breasts can be tortured separately from the rest of her body is a male fantasy related to males' tendency to segment women into "tits, cunts, and asses." The tightness of the rope around the breasts of the woman in the bottom picture must cause considerable pain and humiliation. These three pictures constitute visual evidence of sexual abuse and degradation by the pornographers responsible.

Comment 80. A black woman's cheek is being pinched by a C-clamp in the upper right photograph of this page of a bondage magazine. In the photos on the left, a man is pinching her nipple with a kitchen tong. Use of ordinary household items teaches viewers that they, too, can easily perform such torture at home.

80. Chair Bondage,
vol. 1, no. 1.

81. Source unknown.

83

Comment 81. No parts of a woman's body appear to be exempt from some kind of bondage. In this case it is the woman's head that is most heavily bound. Presumably, providing novelty is the challenge that pornographers have to meet to keep consumers purchasing new copies of expensive magazines. There is absolutely nothing the woman in this photograph can do to control how badly the man pinches her nipple with his pliers. Since her mouth is bound shut, she cannot tell him if the pain is unbearable. Nor can she communicate with her eyes, as they too are covered.

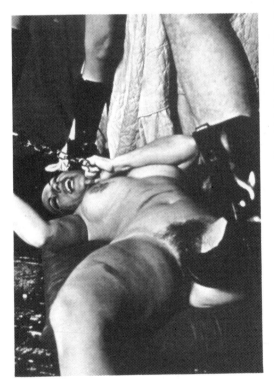

82. Shackled, Vol 1, No. 1.

Comment 82. The woman in this photograph appears distraught. She is grappling with a chain around her neck as a man wearing boots kicks her genitals. Large bruises are visible on her right thigh and stomach. Of course, we cannot be sure that the bruises are real, though it seems unlikely that hard-core pornographers employ skilled make-up artists. We also know from the testimony of women who have been used in pornography that many of them have been tortured in these situations (see *Public Hearings,* 1983; Russell, 1993a).

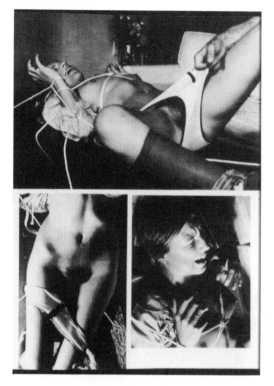

83. Source unknown.

Comment 83. This three-photo sequence shows a woman in bondage having her panties pulled off, then crying with a look of real agony on her face. Rape is implied but not shown. There is no way of knowing whether or not this woman was actually raped that day. It would be difficult to believe that she didn't feel degraded. But whatever she felt, the aim of the pornographer here appears to be to turn male consumers on to the rape implied.

84. Housewives' Horror, unknown bondage magazine.

Comment 84. This is the first page of a six-page photo essay, the goal of which seems to be to eroticize — for males — the idea of breaking into the home of a strange woman, torturing, then raping and sodomizing her. Notice how the text on the first page implies that the woman wanted to be attacked, although the euphemism "action" is used instead of rape: "She was a housewife who needed action." Predictably, the victim is portrayed as succumbing to the sexual excitement of the attack: "There wasn't anything she wouldn't do if he put enough pressure on her. She didn't want to respond, but her juicy cunt gave her away. He knew she'd never tell — she liked it too much!" This is the entire text of this lurid nineteen-photo male fantasy.

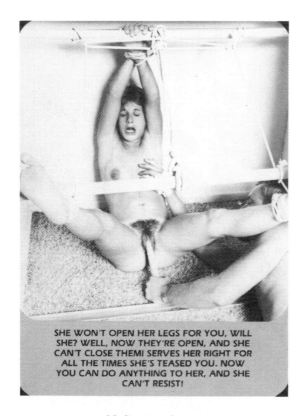

85. Source unknown.

Comment 85. This is a photograph of rape with a foreign object. The message of the text is that when a man feels "teased" by a woman who doesn't wish to have intercourse with him, it is justifiable for him to tie her up and do anything he wants to her, including rape.

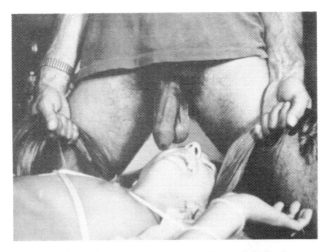

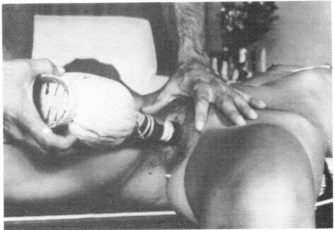

86. Source unknown.

Comment 86. The same woman appears in both these photographs. The rope with which she is bound is more evident in the top photo. Her persecutor is pulling her hair, contributing to the impression that the pornographer wants to convey that she is about to be forced to perform fellatio. In the bottom photo, rape with a wine bottle appears imminent. Whether or not the woman is really about to be raped in both photos, we do not know. We *do* know that some customers require pictures of forced sex in order to become aroused.

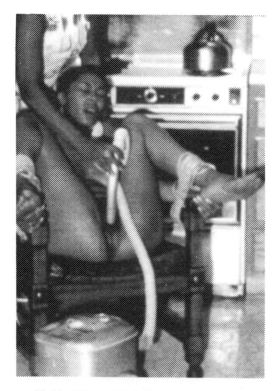

87. Black Tit And Body Torture, vol. 1, no. 1.

Comment 87. This photograph appears in a magazine devoted to the torture of African American women. While the woman is bound and helpless, someone is covering her clitoris with the nozzle of a vacuum cleaner. We do not know whether or not the vacuum cleaner is turned on. If it is, it could well be a very unpleasant and painful experience. The use of a vacuum cleaner on the genitals of an African American woman may also reflect the racist association of black female sexuality with dirt.

Comment 88. This two-page photo essay introduces the woman to be raped this way: "Sally hated waiting for the bus — she was a hot juicy young bitch who couldn't stand the boredom. She was always ready for a good time, especially if the good time was a rough one." "Sally" is depersonalized by the term "bitch" and portrayed as wanting men to be violent toward her. This enables male viewers to see her as responsible for what follows and/or to feel justified in enjoying their own violent sexual fantasies about her.

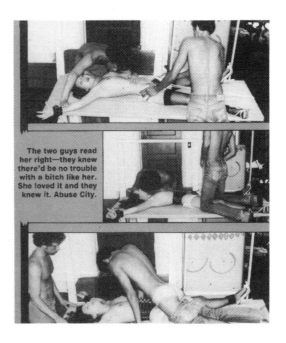

88. *Source unknown.*

Two men accost Sally and start feeling her genitals. In the top picture on page 2, Sally's legs are spread-eagled and she is bound to the four corners of a table while one of the men kisses her left nipple (the contact between his mouth and her nipple is clearly not simulated). The next pictures show her being attacked by both men. As in so much pornography, Sally is nude but for stockings, garter belt and high heels. Only in the last picture does a man bare his ass; this is the double standard of nudity that prevails in much pornography.

Once again, we do not know whether or not the rape in the final photograph was real or simulated. We *do* know that "Sally" was in no position to prevent the rape if it was real. The police would almost certainly discount a rape that occurred in such a setting, since they too would probably hold the victim responsible.

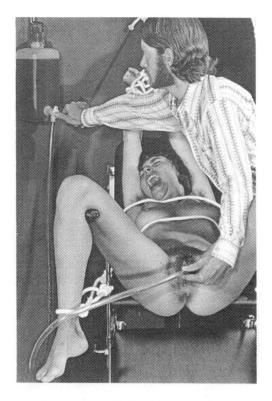

89. Rape 2

Comment 89-91. These three photos are from a magazine which I acquired in Copenhagen in 1974. The text is in English and German. A label informs the reader in four languages that "We send magazines, photos, books, films, etc. all over the world. Write to us and ask for our illustrated catalogue free of charge." The description "High Class Pornography" graces the cover.

These photos do not appear to be simulated and provide evidence that a woman was raped with an enema-like tube filled with red liquid, and (in an unreproduced photo) with a speculum. Following are a few excerpts that depict the real and simulated torture that this woman was put through to produce this photo essay.

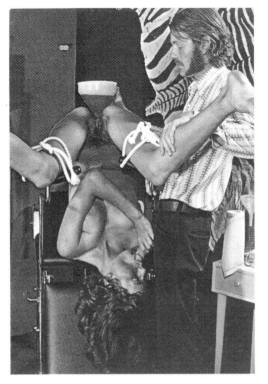

90. Rape 2

The accompanying text reads: "Once more a woman was utterly in his power. He felt an overwhelming urge to abuse the girl, to humiliate her as grossly as possible, to reduce her to a heap of shit.... A tortured scream tore the silence of the chamber.... This reddish liquid, which burned so terribly, filled her cunt with flames.... The effect of the liquid was roughly equivalent to the bites of a hundred ants. Ecstatically Karl exulted in the indescribable agonies of the girl.... She was totally burnt-out and had cracked up under the strain of the mental torture she had been subjected to.... He swelled with pride that he seemed to have broken her will completely.... She really was nothing but a bundle of agonized nerves, completely broken down, degraded and debased."

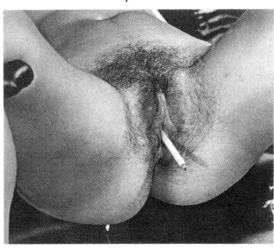

91. Rape 2

Comment 91. The text under the third photo reads: "Karl, however, had much more in store for her. 'Now I need a short pause,' he said, leering at her, 'then we can go on!... The break will just be long enough for a fag,' he said." After putting a burning cigarette up her vagina, Karl tells her, " 'You can call me when it burns.' "

92. Chic magazine.

Comment 92. The largest of these three photographs shows a woman called "Columbine" stabbing herself in the vagina with a large knife. This bloody act of self-mutilation does not wipe the smile off her face. The top photo on the right portrays Columbine cutting off a section off her labia with scissors. In the bottom one she is cutting off one of her nipples. The text under these photos reads as follows: "Columbine, who stars in an off-off-off Broadway Company has a penchant for the self-destructive and self-mutilative.... 'I would much rather masturbate with a knife than a dildo,' says Columbine.... 'I guess because I've always had an inferiority complex, I think of myself as deserving to be stabbed and killed.' "

93. Hustler, vol. 1, 1984.

Comment 93. This photograph is from a ten-page photo essay called "Danielle: the Bear Facts." By the end of the story, the bear is licking her lower stomach and the woman is feigning being sexually excited by this. I would like to know what she was really feeling. Very frightened, I imagine. I would think that no matter how tame the bear, being so close to it would be dangerous for her. If my surmise is correct, it follows that her life was placed at risk for men's sexual entertainment.

94. Animal Love.

Comment 94. The next two photographs appeared in a booklet I acquired in Copenhagen, Denmark in 1974. Most of the pornography stores there had a section devoted to women having sex with animals. These stores were not confined to the sleazy parts of town, but on the contrary, were to be found in well-to-do areas frequented by many tourists. This picture shows a pig's penis penetrating a resigned-looking woman's vagina. This is clearly no simulated photograph.

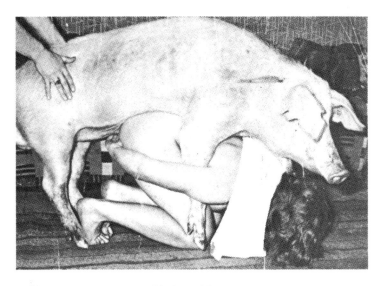

95. Animal Love.

Comment 95. This picture shows the woman plus another person trying to position the pig to effect vaginal penetration. Other pictures in this booklet show the pig's snout and mouth in the woman's genitals, and the woman giving the pig's penis an open mouthed kiss.

The next sixteen photographs provide examples of pornography depicting sexual femicide (the misogynist killing of women by males for sexual gratification). Of all the kinds of power one person can wield over another, the ultimate is the power of life and death. In these pictures, the death, murder, and mutilation of women are eroticized.

96. Snuff Poster, 1979.

Comment 96. This is a poster advertising a film which imitates the notorious Snuff movie in which a woman was tortured, mutilated and killed. In the final scene, a man rips out a woman's uterus and holds it up in the air while he ejaculates.

The blurb next to the word "Snuff" on this poster reads: "The *bloodiest* thing that *ever* happened in front of a camera." Although the murder portrayed in "Snuff" was simulated by trick photography, its fakery was apparently difficult to ascertain. In order for snuff movies to have become a marketable genre in the pornography industry, a significant number of males must find it sexually arousing to witness a woman being murdered and disembowelled, or to witness the realistic simulation of these activities. This is a terrifying and macabre reality for women in the United States where so many have been killed or threatened by woman-hating strangers, work mates, boy friends, and husbands.

Comment 97. The text in this picture reads, "A man who gets what he deserves is considered to have received his 'just desserts.' Here are a few sweet rewards as composed by photographer Steve Allison. One would be hard put to find a more delicious ending to any meal...or a lovelier stimulant to whet a rather different form of appetite."

This picture is part of a series in which women's breasts are depicted as various foods. This one, called "Peaches 'n' Cream," shows a severed breast in a pie tin surrounded by peaches. The bottom line states that these photos are available as posters.

97. Gallery, January 1980.

98. *Hustler, June 1978.*

Comment 98. Feminists have frequently protested that women in pornography are treated like pieces of meat. As this cover picture demonstrates, Larry Flynt used this charge as a pretext to escalate the assault on women. Although his taunt, "We will no longer hang women up like pieces of meat," sounds like an unexpected concession to feminists, the picture of a woman being ground up in a meat grinder is a graphic image of his crudity, hatred and violence.

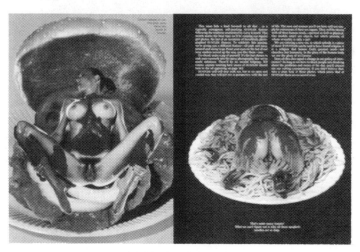

99. Hustler, June 1978.

Comment 99. These two pictures appeared inside the woman-in-a-meat-grinder cover issue. An excerpt from the text reads, "Grilled indoors or out, this pink patty takes two hands to handle." Here Flynt carries the "woman as meat" joke further — into slicing women up and eating them (cannibalism). Imagine the public outcry there would be if similar pictures of black men were published in a non-pornographic magazine produced by white Americans, or by white South Africans.

100. "The Best of Hustler," Hustler, 1979.

Comment 100. This photograph is from a photo story entitled, "The Naked and the Dead." In the first scene, a nude woman is led from a cell by fully dressed guards. In the next, she is shown having her head shaved — an act reminiscent of the shaving of inmates' heads in Nazi concentration camps. In this photo, the woman's pubic hair is being shaved off while she is sprawled naked and in handcuffs. A male guard rapes her in a subsequent photo. The final picture is blank except for the word "POOF!" in large letters, suggesting that the woman was killed.

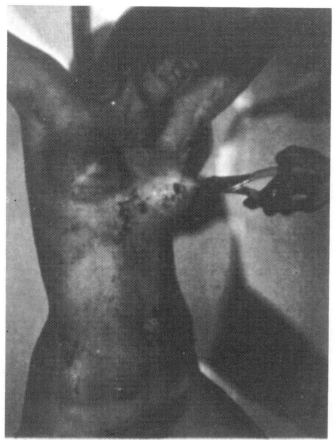

SNUFF LIB
e incredible and mysterious saga of a film none of us
ill ever see. By CHERI's resident master of gore.

101. Cheri.

Comment 101. This photograph looks even more hideous in color than it does in black and white, since the blood all over this woman's body is much more visible. The term "Snuff Lib" (a warning and putdown of women's liberation) implies a call to men who enjoy killing women to come out of the closet to act out their murderous desires. It also suggests that snuff libbers have been oppressed by having to remain in the closet. The meaning of the caption: "The incredible and mysterious saga of a film none of us will ever see," is more obscure. Perhaps it means that no men (clearly "us" does not include women) will ever be able to see it because — as a record of murder — it is too dangerous to distribute, even underground.

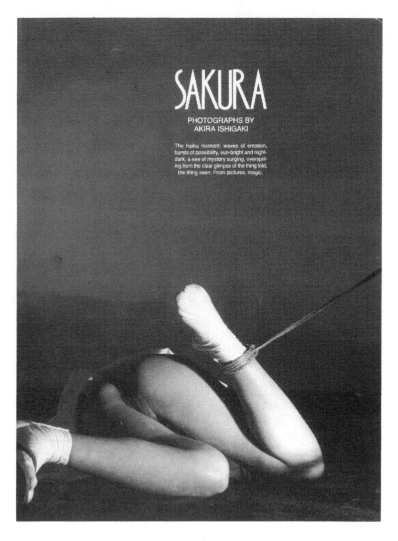

102. Penthouse, December 1984.

These pictures (102–104) are three of eleven photographs from a photo essay entitled *"Sakura"* that appeared in a "Holiday Issue" of *Penthouse* magazine. A classic Japanese poetry form, the haiku, accompanies the photos in an attempt to provide the pictures with artistic credibility. Photographer Akira Ishigaki describes the meaning of the title as follows: *"Sakura* is the word for the cherry blossom. From my childhood...I recall the resemblance between the petals of the cherry blossom and a woman's body. In the spring of my twelve years, I caressed the petals with my fingers, kissed them gently with my lips." Ishigaki's sensitive and subtle verbiage contrasts dramatically with the brutal, femicidal photographs that eroticize the torture, bondage, hanging, and death of young Japanese women. The implicit message of this series is that the portrayal of brutality toward women is acceptable when it meets society's artistic standards.

103. Penthouse, December 1984.

Comment 102. The photograph of the title page of this photo essay shows a girl or woman on a rocky coastal bluff with one ankle bound, the rope held taut, suggesting an unseen captor. The suggestion of an unseen captor places the male viewer in that role. Her pubic hair and leg hair have been shaved off, contributing to the glamorization of her plight. Shaving recreates the woman as child, increasing her vulnerability and, hence, her desirability. (Imagine how hairy legs would de-eroticize this image.)

Comment 103. The woman/girl in this picture appears to be dead. The photographer has used his skills to glamorize and eroticize a female corpse. It seems probable that pictures like this (and the last one) contribute to eroticizing necrophilia, or intensifying the erotic response to it in those males who already find it a turn on.

104. Penthouse, December 1984.

Comment 104. This photograph shows a woman in a harness suspended by a rope from a tree. She seems to be unconscious or dead, her body limp and her head slumped forward. This image is reminiscent of the lynching of African Americans. Two months after this issue of *Penthouse* appeared on the stands, Jean Kar-Har Fewel, an eight-year-old Chinese girl living in North Carolina, was found raped and murdered, tied to a tree with ropes around her neck. Many feminists believe that *Penthouse* owner Bob Guccione is in part responsible for her horrifying death. Ishigaki's delicate prose and technically beautiful photography contribute to making the vicious content of these pictures more acceptable, thereby serving to legitimize the violence against women portrayed.

105. "Maniac," movie ad.

Comment 105. For women, the message of "Maniac" is that if they don't obey men's warnings, their lives are at risk. For males, the message is that if women don't obey their orders, they are entitled to punish them, perhaps even kill them. Although viewers know that they are watching a movie, not a documentary, research shows that there are significant changes in males' attitudes toward females, and about rape, after watching such movies (see Part 2).

The ad for "Maniac" looks more garish in color, with pools and splatterings of blood everywhere. There are many such ads and films, but this is the only example of a woman-slashing movie included in this book. Although there is no nudity in this particular ad, these films invariably use full or partial female nudity, sexually suggestive poses, and a wide array of brutal images of violence against women. This combination serves to sexualize violence against women. Although some people make a big distinction between these films and pornography, they meet the definition of pornography presented in the introduction to this book. I believe that these examples of soft-core snuff movies are extremely dangerous to women and girls.

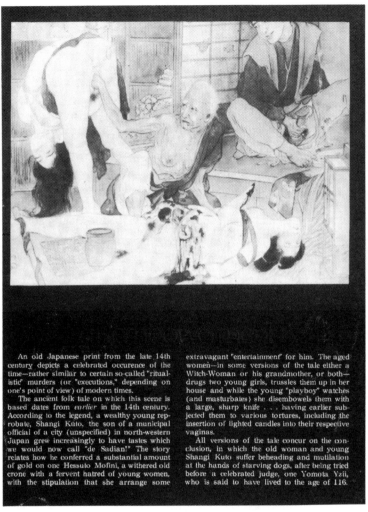

An old Japanese print from the late 14th century depicts a celebrated occurence of the time—rather similar to certain so-called "ritual-istic" murders (or "executions," depending on one's point of view) of modern times.

The ancient folk tale on which this scene is based dates from earlier in the 14th century. According to the legend, a wealthy young reprobate, Shangi Kuto, the son of a municipal official of a city (unspecified) in north-western Japan grew increasingly to have tastes which we would now call "de Sadian!" The story relates how he conferred a substantial amount of gold on one Hessuto Mofini, a withered old crone with a fervent hatred of young women, with the stipulation that she arrange some

extravagant "entertainment" for him. The aged women—in some versions of the tale either a Witch-Woman or his grandmother, or both—drugs two young girls, trusses them up in her house and while the young "playboy" watches (and masturbates) she disembowels them with a large, sharp knife . . . having earlier subjected them to various tortures, including the insertion of lighted candles into their respective vaginas.

All versions of the tale concur on the conclusion, in which the old woman and young Shangi Kuto suffer beheading and mutilation at the hands of starving dogs, after being tried before a celebrated judge, one Yomota Yzii, who is said to have lived to the age of 116.

106. *A Garden of Pain*. WAVPM display.

Comment 106. This is a photograph of an old Japanese print from the late 14th century titled "Disembowelment" that was republished in a Japanese magazine on sadomasochism. According to the text, this print depicts "a celebrated occurrence of the time — rather similar to certain so-called 'ritualistic' murders...of modern times.... According to the legend, a wealthy young reprobate...grew increasingly to have tastes which we would now call 'de Sadian!' The story relates how he conferred a substantial amount of gold on one Hessuto Mofini, a withered old crone with a fervent hatred of young women, with the stipulation that she arrange some extravagant 'entertainment' for him. The aged women...drugs two young girls, trusses them up in her house and, while the young 'playboy' watches (and masturbates), she disembowels them with a large, sharp knife...having earlier subjected them to various tortures, including the insertion of lighted candles into their respective vaginas."

Comment 107. This is another 14th century Japanese print, one of the most gruesome pictures I have ever seen. Notice the two mutilated women's corpses hanging by the feet in the background, and the man's torture implements in the foreground. The corpse of the woman the man is still mutilating reveals that the victim was tied up with her arms behind her and her legs spread-eagled. Long needles protrude from her neck, some kind of torture implement has been stuck up her anus, her shins have been cut open. With his right hand, the man is tearing off the corpse's nipples, while with the left he has plunged a sword into her vagina so far that it exits through her stomach. Although the original is a drawing, not a photograph, this depiction of a Japanese Jack-the-Ripper may have inspired other males to imitate the abominable acts he appears to enjoy.

107. *A Garden of Pain.* WAVPM display.

108. Hustler, June 1990.

Comment 108. This picture also ranks as one of the most barbaric I have ever seen. Four pictures of women's bodies are attached with razor blades to what appears to be human skin. Also fastened to the skin are clitorises and nipples with fish hooks and safety pins through them. Some of the skin, which is stapled or hooked together, is burned. The picture on the top left depicts a decapitated woman with severed hands. The middle picture shows a woman whose left leg is blown away, her trunk ripped open. A knife is at her side. The top right picture is splattered with blood and portrays a dead woman by a toilet. The bottom picture shows the severed trunk of a woman whose legs are also amputated below the knees.

Rape, battery, and murder are criminal offenses in the United States and elsewhere. Yet the portrayal of these crimes against women is a popular form of entertainment for U.S. males. Millions of males regularly ejaculate to degrading pictures of women. This in turn intensifies their sexual response to women being abused. It is this sexual component, including the sexual gratification involved, that sets pornography apart from non-pornographic depictions that are degrading and/or violent toward women, and which makes pornography particularly dangerous.

That it is considered acceptable to treat women in the ways photographed here implies more than a tolerance of, and desensitization to, women's pain and degradation. It constitutes a massive hate crime against women as a gender. Would males be so cavalier about pornography, labelling it as mere free speech, if instead of the rape of women by men, pornography celebrated women cutting off men's penises and testicles? Societies that call themselves civilized cannot at the same time continue tolerating pornography's invitation to men to rape, abuse, mutilate and kill women.

As Andrea Dworkin and Catharine MacKinnon have stated: "The pornographers have convinced many that *their* freedom is everyone's freedom" (1988, emphasis added). Elsewhere, Dworkin points out: "In defending pornography, as if it were speech, liberals defend the new slavers."

PART 2

PORNOGRAPHY
AS A CAUSE OF RAPE

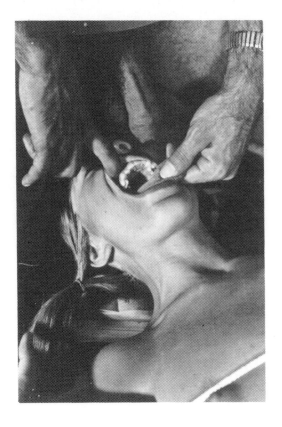

Source unknown

INTRODUCTION:

PORNOGRAPHY AS VIOLENCE AGAINST WOMEN

"I don't need studies and statistics to tell me that there is a relationship between pornography and real violence against women. My body re-
members." — *Woman's testimony, 1983.*[1]

"The relationship between particularly sexually violent images in the media and subsequent aggression...is much stronger statistically than the relationship between smoking and lung cancer."
— *Edward Donnerstein, 1983.*

When addressing the question of whether or not pornography causes rape, as well as other forms of sexual assault and violence, many people fail to acknowledge that the actual *making* of pornography some-times involves, or even requires, violence and sexual assault. Testimony by women and men involved in such activity provide numerous examples of this (*Public Hearings*, 1983; *Attorney General's Commission*, 1986).

In one case, a man who said he had participated in over a hundred pornographic movies testified at the Commission hearings in Los Angeles as follows: "I, myself, have been on a couple of sets where the young ladies have been forced to do even anal sex scenes with a guy which [sic] is rather large and I have seen them crying in pain" (1986, p. 773).

Another witness testified at the Los Angeles hearings as follows:

Women and young girls were tortured and suffered permanent physical injuries to answer publisher demands for photographs depicting sado-

---

1   This survivor of pornography-related incestuous abuse testified at the Minneapolis Hearings on pornography *(Public Hearings, 1983).*

masochistic abuse. When the torturer/photographer inquired of the publisher as to the types of depictions that would sell, the torturer/photographer was instructed to get similar existing publications and use the depiction therein for instruction. The torturer/photographer followed the publisher's instructions, tortured women and girls accordingly, and then sold the photographs to the publisher. The photographs were included in magazines sold nationally in pornographic outlets (1986, pp. 787-788).

Peter Bogdanovich writes of *Playboy* "Playmate of the Year" Dorothy Stratten's response to her participation in a pornographic movie: "A key sequence in *Galaxina* called for Dorothy to be spread-eagled against a cold water tower. The producers insisted she remain bound there for several hours, day and night. In one shot of the completed film, the tears she cries are real" (1984, p. 59). Although this movie was not made for the so-called adult movie houses, I consider it pornography because of its sexist and degrading combination of sexuality and bondage.

A letter was sent to the United States Attorney General's Commission on Pornography reporting that: "A mother and father in South Oklahoma City forced their four daughters, ages ten to seventeen, to engage in family sex while pornographic pictures were being filmed" (1986, p. 780).

It should not be assumed that violence occurs only in the making of violent pornography. For example, although many people would classify the movie *Deep Throat* as non-violent pornography because it does not portray rape or other violence, we now know from Linda (Lovelace) Marchiano's two books (*Ordeal*, 1980, and *Out of Bondage*, 1986), as well as from her public testimony (for example, *Public Hearings*, 1983), that this film is in fact a documentary of her rape from beginning to end.

Many people, including some of the best researchers on pornography in this country, ignore the violence used by pornographers in the manufacturing of these misogynist materials (for example, see Malamuth and Donnerstein, 1984). Catharine MacKinnon points out the frequently forgotten fact that "before pornography became the pornographer's speech it was somebody's life" (1987, p. 179). Testimony presented at the hearings held on the anti-pornography civil rights ordinance in Minneapolis, Minnesota in 1983, provides powerful evidence for the truth of this statement (*Public Hearings*, 1983; Russell, 1993a).

Because it is important to know the proclivities and the state of mind of those who read and view pornography, I will start by discussing some of the data on males' propensity to rape.

MALES' PROPENSITY TO RAPE[2]

"Why do I want to rape women? Because I am basically, as a male, a predator and all women look to men like prey. I fantasize about the expression on a woman's face when I 'capture' her and she realizes she cannot escape. It's like I won, I own her."

— *Male respondent, Shere Hite, 1981, p. 718.*

Research indicates that 25% to 30% of male college students in the United States and Canada admit that there is some likelihood they would rape a woman if they could get away with it.[3] In the first study of males' self-reported likelihood to rape that was conducted at the University of California at Los Angeles, the word *rape* was not used; instead, an account of rape (described below) was read to the male subjects, of whom 53% said there was some likelihood that they would behave in the same fashion as the man described in the story, if they could be sure of getting away with it (Malamuth, Haber, and Feshbach, 1980). Without this assurance, only 17% said they might emulate the rapist's behavior. It is helpful to know exactly what behavior these students said they might emulate:

> Bill soon caught up with Susan and offered to escort her to her car. Susan politely refused him. Bill was enraged by the rejection. "Who the hell does this bitch think she is, turning me down," Bill thought to himself as he reached into his pocket and took out a Swiss army knife. With his left hand he placed the knife at her throat. "If you try to get away, I'll cut you," said Bill. Susan nodded her head, her eyes wild with terror.
>
> The story then depicted the rape. There was a description of sexual acts with the victim continuously portrayed as clearly opposing the assault (Malamuth, Haber, and Feshbach, 1980, p. 124).

In another study, 356 male students were asked: "If you could be assured that no one would know and that you could in no way be punished for engaging in the following acts, how likely, if at all, would you

---

2   I use the term *males* rather than *men* because many rapists are juveniles.
3   In 1984 Malamuth reported that in several studies an average of about 35% of male students indicated some likelihood of raping a woman (1984, p. 22). This figure has decreased to 25% to 30% since then, for reasons Malamuth cannot explain (personal communication, July 1986).

be to commit such acts?" (Briere and Malamuth, 1983). Among the sexual acts listed were the two of interest to these researchers: "forcing a female to do something she really didn't want to do" and "rape" (Briere and Malamuth, 1983). *Sixty percent of the sample indicated that under the right circumstances, there was some likelihood that they would rape, use force, or do both.*

In a study of high school males, 50% of those interviewed believed it acceptable "for a guy to hold a girl down and force her to have sexual intercourse in instances such as when 'she gets him sexually excited' or 'she says she's going to have sex with him and then changes her mind' " (Goodchilds and Zellman, 1984).

Some people dismiss the findings from these studies as "merely attitudinal." But this conclusion is incorrect. Malamuth has found that male subjects' self-reported likelihood of raping is correlated with physiological measures of sexual arousal by rape depictions. Clearly, erections cannot be considered attitudes. More specifically, the male students who say they might rape a woman if they could get away with it are significantly more likely than other male students to be sexually aroused by portrayals of rape. Indeed, these males were more sexually aroused by depictions of rape than by mutually consenting depictions. And when asked if they would find committing a rape sexually arousing, they said yes (Donnerstein, 1983, p. 7). They were also more likely than the other male subjects to admit to having used actual physical force to obtain sex with a woman. These latter data were self-reported, but because they refer to actual behavior they too cannot be dismissed as merely attitudinal.

Looking at sexual arousal data alone (as measured by penile tumescence), not its correlation with self-reported likelihood to rape, Malamuth reports that:

- About 10% of the population of male students are sexually aroused by "very extreme violence" with "a great deal of blood and gore" that "has very little of the sexual element" (1985, p. 95).

- About 20% to 30% show substantial sexual arousal by depictions of rape in which the woman never shows signs of arousal, only abhorrence (1985, p. 95).

- About 50% to 60% show some degree of sexual arousal by a rape depiction in which the victim is portrayed as becoming sexually aroused at the end (personal communication, August 18, 1986).

Given these findings, it is hardly surprising that after reviewing a whole series of related experiments, Neil Malamuth concluded that "the overall pattern of the data is...consistent with contentions that many men have a proclivity to rape" (1981b, p. 139).

Shere Hite (1981, p. 1123) provides data on men's self-reported desire to rape women from the general population outside the university laboratory. Distinguishing between those men who answered the question anonymously and those who revealed their identities, Hite reports the following answers by the anonymous group to her question "Have you ever wanted to rape a woman?": 46% answered "yes" or "sometimes," 47% answered "no," and 7% said they had fantasies of rape, but presumably had not acted them out — yet (1981, p. 1123).

Surprisingly, the non-anonymous group of men reported slightly more interest in rape: 52% answered "yes" or "sometimes," 36% answered "no," and 11% reported having rape fantasies. (Could it be that many men don't think there is anything wrong with wanting to rape women?) Although Hite's survey was not based on a random sample, and therefore, like the experimental work cited above, cannot be generalized to the population at large, her finding that roughly half of the more than 7,000 men she surveyed admitted to having wanted to rape a woman on one or more occasions suggests that men's propensity to rape is probably very widespread indeed. It is interesting that Hite's percentages are comparable to my finding that 44% of a probability sample of 930 adult women residing in San Francisco reported having been the victim of one or more rapes or attempted rapes over the course of their lives (Russell, 1984).

The studies reviewed here suggest that at this time in the history of our culture, a substantial percentage of the male population has some desire or proclivity to rape females. Indeed, some males in this culture consider themselves deviant for *not* wanting to rape a woman. For example, the answer of one of Hite's male respondents was: "I have never raped a woman, or wanted to. In this I guess *I am somewhat odd*. Many of my friends talk about rape a lot and fantasize about it. The whole idea leaves me cold" (1981, p. 719; emphasis added). Another replied: "I must admit a certain part of me would receive some sort of thrill at ripping the clothes from a woman and ravishing her. But I would probably collapse into tears of pity and weep with my victim, *unlike the traditional man*" (1981, p. 719; emphasis added).

Some feminists are among the optimists who believe that males' proclivity to rape is largely a consequence of social and cultural forces, not biological ones. And, of course, having a *desire* to behave in a certain way is not the same as actually *behaving* in that way, particularly in the case of antisocial behavior. Nevertheless, it is helpful to have this kind of baseline information on the desires and predispositions of males, who are, after all, the chief consumers of pornography.

A THEORY ABOUT
THE CAUSATIVE ROLE OF PORNOGRAPHY

Sociologist David Finkelhor has developed a very useful multicausal theory to explain the occurrence of child sexual abuse (1984). According to Finkelhor's model, in order for child sexual abuse to occur, four conditions have to be met. First, someone has to *want* to abuse a child sexually. Second, this person's internal inhibitions against acting out this desire have to be undermined. Third, this person's social inhibitions against acting out this desire (e.g., fear of being caught and punished) have to be undermined. Fourth, the would-be perpetrator has to undermine or overcome his or her chosen victim's capacity to avoid or resist the sexual abuse.

According to my theory, these conditions also have to be met in order for rape, battery, and other forms of sexual assault on adult women to occur (Russell, 1984). Although my theory can be applied to other forms of sexual abuse and violence against women besides rape, the following formulation of it will focus on rape because most of the research relevant to my theory is limited to this form of sexual assault.

In *Sexual Exploitation* (1984) I suggest many factors that may predispose a large number of males in the United States to want to rape or assault women sexually. Some examples discussed in this book are (1) biological factors, (2) childhood experiences of sexual abuse, (3) male sex-role socialization, (4) exposure to mass media that encourage rape, and (5) exposure to pornography. Here I will discuss only the role of pornography.

Although women have been known to rape both males and females, males are by far the predominant perpetrators of sexual assault as well as the biggest consumers of pornography. Hence, my theory will focus on male perpetrators.

A diagrammatic presentation of this theory appears in Figure 1. As previously noted, in order for rape to occur, a man must not only be predisposed to rape, but his internal and social inhibitions against acting out his rape desires must be undermined. My theory, in a nutshell, is that pornography (1) predisposes some males to want to rape women and intensifies the predisposition in other males already so predisposed; (2) undermines some males' internal inhibitions against acting out their desire to rape; and (3) undermines some males' social inhibitions against acting out their desire to rape.

THE MEANING OF "CAUSE"

Given the intense debate about whether or not pornography plays a causal role in rape, it is surprising that so few of those engaged in it ever state what they mean by "cause." A definition of the concept of *simple causation* follows:

> An event (or events) that precedes and results in the occurrence of another event. Whenever the first event (the cause) occurs, the second event (the effect) necessarily or inevitably follows. Moreover, in simple causation the second event does not occur unless the first event has occurred. Thus the cause is both the SUFFICIENT CONDITION and the NECESSARY CONDITION for the occurrence of the effect (Theodorson and Theodorson, 1979).

By this definition, pornography clearly does not cause rape, as it seems safe to assume that some pornography consumers do not rape women, and that many rapes are unrelated to pornography. However, the concept of *multiple causation is* applicable to the relationship between pornography and rape.

> With the conception of MULTIPLE CAUSATION, various possible causes may be seen for a given event, any one of which may be a sufficient but not necessary condition for the occurrence of the effect, or a necessary but not sufficient condition. In the case of multiple causation, then, the given effect may occur in the absence of all but one of the possible sufficient but not necessary causes; and, conversely, the given effect would not follow the occurrence of some but not all of

Theoretical Model of Pornogra

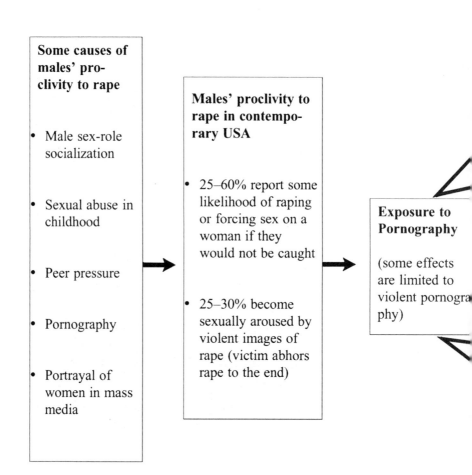

Some causes of males' proclivity to rape	Males' proclivity to rape in contemporary USA	Exposure to Pornography
• Male sex-role socialization	• 25–60% report some likelihood of raping or forcing sex on a woman if they would not be caught	(some effects are limited to violent pornogra phy)
• Sexual abuse in childhood		
• Peer pressure	• 25–30% become sexually aroused by violent images of rape (victim abhors rape to the end)	
• Pornography		
• Portrayal of women in mass media		

Figure 1

ls a Cause of Rape

FACTOR I.   **PREDISPOSES SOME MALES TO DESIRE RAPE OR INTENSIFIES THIS DESIRE**

1. by pairing sexually arousing stimuli with portrayals of rape
2. by becoming sexually aroused by self-generated rape fantasies
3. by sexualizing dominance and submission
4. by creating an appetite for increasingly stronger material

FACTOR II.   **UNDERMINES SOME MALES' INTERNAL INHIBITIONS AGAINST ACTING OUT RAPE DESIRES**

1. by sexually objectifying females
2. by increasing belief in rape myths
3. by increasing acceptance of interpersonal violence
4. by increasing trivialization of rape
5. by increasing sex-callous attitudes and hostility to women
6. by increasing acceptance of male dominance in intimate relationships
7. by desensitizing males to rape and violence against women

FACTOR III.   **UNDERMINES SOME MALES' SOCIAL INHIBITIONS AGAINST ACTING OUT RAPE DESIRES**

1. by diminishing fears of social sanctions
2. by diminishing fear that peers will disapprove

FACTOR IV.   **UNDERMINES SOME POTENTIAL VICTIMS' ABILITIES TO AVOID OR RESIST RAPE**

1. by encouraging females to get into high rape-risk situations
2. by creating a pornography industry that requires female participation

the various necessary but not sufficient causes (Theodorson and Theo-dorson, 1979).

As I have already presented the research on males' proclivity to rape, I will next discuss some of the evidence that pornography can be a sufficient (though not *necessary*) condition for males to desire to rape (see the list on the far right of Figure 1). I will mention when the research findings I describe apply to violent pornography and when to pornography that appears to the viewer to be non-violent.

I. THE ROLE OF PORNOGRAPHY IN PREDISPOSING SOME MALES TO WANT TO RAPE

"I went to a porno bookstore, put a quarter in a slot, and saw this porn movie. It was just a guy coming up from behind a girl and attacking her and raping her. That's when I started having rape fantasies. When I seen that movie, it was like somebody lit a fuse from my childhood on up.... I just went for it, went out and raped." (Rapist interviewed by Beneke, 1982, pp. 73-74.)

According to Factor I in my theoretical model, pornography can induce a desire to rape women in males who previously had no such desire, and it can increase or intensify the desire to rape in males who already have felt this desire. This section will provide the evidence for the four different ways in which pornography can induce this predisposition that are listed alongside Factor I in Figure 1.

(1) *Pairing sexually arousing/gratifying stimuli with rape*

The laws of social learning (for example, classical conditioning, instrumental conditioning, and social modelling), about which there is now considerable consensus among psychologists, apply to all the mass media, including pornography. As Donnerstein testified at the hearings in Minneapolis: "If you assume that your child can learn from Sesame Street how to count one, two, three, four, five, believe me, they can learn how to pick up a gun" (Donnerstein, 1983, p. 11). Presumably, males can learn equally well how to rape, beat, sexually abuse, and degrade females.

A simple application of the laws of social learning suggests that viewers of pornography can develop arousal responses to depictions of rape, murder, child sexual abuse, or other assaultive behavior. Researcher S. Rachman of the Institute of Psychiatry, Maudsley Hospital, London, has demonstrated that male subjects can learn to become sexually aroused by seeing a picture of a woman's boot after repeatedly seeing women's boots in association with sexually arousing slides of nude females (Rachman and Hodgson, 1968). The laws of learning that operated in the acquisition of the boot fetish can also teach males who were not previously aroused by depictions of rape to become so. All it may take is the repeated association of rape with arousing portrayals of female nudity (or clothed females in provocative poses).

Even for males who are not sexually excited during movie portrayals of rape, masturbation subsequent to the movie reinforces the association. This constitutes what R. J. McGuire, J. M. Carlisle and B. G. Young refer to as "masturbatory conditioning" (Cline, 1974, p. 210). The pleasurable experience of orgasm — an expected and planned-for activity in many pornography parlours — is an exceptionally potent reinforcer. The fact that pornography is widely used by males as ejaculation material is a major factor that differentiates it from other mass media, intensifying the lessons that males consumers learn from it.

(2) *Increasing males' self-generated rape fantasies*

Further evidence that exposure to pornography can create in males a predisposition to rape where none existed before is provided by an experiment conducted by Malamuth. Malamuth classified 29 male students as sexually force-oriented or non-force-oriented on the basis of their responses to a questionnaire (1981a). These students were then randomly assigned to view either a rape version or a mutually consenting version of a slide-audio presentation. The account of rape and accompanying pictures were based on a story in a popular pornographic magazine, which Malamuth describes as follows:

> The man in this story finds an attractive woman on a deserted road. When he approaches her, she faints with fear. In the rape version, the man ties her up and forcibly undresses her. The accompanying narrative is as follows: "You take her into the car. Though this experience is new to you, there is a temptation too powerful to resist. When she awakens, you tell her she had better do exactly as you say or she'll be sorry. With terrified eyes she agrees. She is undressed and she is willing to succumb to whatever you want. You kiss her and she returns the kiss." Portrayal of the man and woman in sexual acts follows; intercourse is implied rather than explicit (1981a, p. 38).

In the mutually consenting version of the story the victim was not tied up or threatened. Instead, on her awakening in the car, the man told her that "she is safe and that no one will do her any harm. She seems to like you and you begin to kiss." The rest of the story is identical to the rape version (Malamuth, 1981a, p. 38).

All subjects were then exposed to the same audio description of a rape read by a female. This rape involved threats with a knife, beatings, and physical restraint. The victim was portrayed as pleading, crying, screaming, and fighting against the rapist (Abel, Barlow, Blanchard, and Guild, 1977, p. 898). Malamuth reports that measures of penile tumescence as well as self-reported arousal "indicated that relatively high levels of sexual arousal were generated by all the experimental stimuli" (1981a, p. 33).

After the 29 male students had been exposed to the rape audio tape, they were asked to try to reach as high a level of sexual arousal as possible by fantasizing about whatever they wanted but without any direct stimulation of the penis (1981a, p. 40). Self-reported sexual arousal during the fantasy period indicated that those students who had been exposed to the rape version of the first slide-audio presentation, created more violent sexual fantasies than those exposed to the mutually consenting version *irrespective of whether they had been classified as force-oriented or non-force-oriented* (1981a, p. 33).

As the rape version of the slide-audio presentation is typical of what is seen in pornography, the results of this experiment suggest that similar pornographic depictions are likely to generate rape fantasies even in previously non-force-oriented consumers. As Edna Einsiedel points out (1986, p. 60):

> Current evidence suggests a high correlation between deviant fantasies and deviant behaviors.... Some treatment methods are also predicated on the link between fantasies and behavior by attempting to alter fantasy patterns in order to change the deviant behaviors (1986, p. 60).

Because so many people resist the idea that a desire to rape may develop as a result of viewing pornography, let us focus for a moment on behavior other than rape. There is abundant testimonial evidence that at least some males decide they would like to perform certain sex acts on women after seeing pornography portraying such sex acts. For example, one of the men who answered Shere Hite's question on pornography wrote: "It's great for me. *It gives me new ideas to try and see*, and it's always sexually exciting" (1981, p. 780; emphasis added). Of course, there's nothing wrong with getting new ideas from pornography or anywhere else, nor with trying them out, as long as they are not actions that subordinate or violate others. Unfortunately, many of the behaviors modelled in pornography *do* subordinate and violate women, sometimes viciously. The following statements were made by women testifying at the Hearing on Pornography in Minneapolis, Minnesota, in 1983 (Russell, 1993a).

Ms. M testified that,

I agreed to act out in private a lot of the scenarios that my husband read to me. These depicted bondage and different sexual acts that I found very humiliating to do.... He read the pornography like a textbook, like a journal. When he finally convinced me to be bound, he read in the magazine how to tie the knots and bind me in a way that I couldn't escape. Most of the scenes where I had to dress up or go through different fantasies were the exact same scenes that he had read in the magazines.

Ms. O described a case in which a man

brought pornographic magazines, books, and paraphernalia into the bedroom with him and told her [his ex-wife] that if she did not perform the sexual acts in the 'dirty' books and magazines, he would beat her and kill her.

Ms. S testifed about the experiences of a group of women prostitutes who, she said,

were forced constantly to enact specific scenes that men had witnessed in pornography.... These men...would set up scenarios, usually with more than one woman, to copy scenes that they had seen portrayed in magazines and books. Then they would make their movies using home video equipment and Polaroid cameras for their own libraries of pornography. [For example, Ms. S. quoted a woman in her group as saying:] "He held up a porn magazine with a picture of a beaten woman and said, 'I want you to look like that. I want you to hurt.' He then began beating me. When I did not cry fast enough, he lit a cigarette and held it right above my breast for a long time before he burned me."

Ms. S also described what three men did to a nude woman prostitute whom they had tied up while she was seated on a chair:

They burned her with cigarettes and attached nipple clips to her breasts. They had many S and M magazines with them and showed her many pictures of women appearing to consent, enjoy, and encourage this abuse. She was held for twelve hours while she was continuously raped and beaten.

Another example cited by Ms. S:

They [several Johns] forced the women to act simultaneously with the movie. In the movie at this point, a group of men were urinating on a naked woman. All the men in the room were able to perform this task, so they all started urninating on the woman who was now naked.

When a male engages in a particularly unusual act that he had previously encountered in pornography, it becomes even more likely that the decision to do so was inspired by the pornography. One woman, for example, testified to the Attorney General's Commission on Pornography about the pornography-related death of her son:

> My son, Troy Daniel Dunaway, was murdered on August 6, 1981, by the greed and avarice of the publishers of *Hustler* magazine. My son read the article "Orgasm of Death," set up the sexual experiment depicted therein, followed the explicit instructions of the article, and ended up dead. He would still be alive today were he not enticed and incited into this action by *Hustler* magazine's "How to Do" August 1981 article, an article which was found at his feet and which directly caused his death (1986, p. 797).

When children do what they see in pornography, it is even more improbable than in the case of adults that their behavior can be attributed entirely to their predispositions.

Psychologist Jennings Bryant testified to the Pornography Commission about a survey he had conducted involving 600 telephone interviews with males and females who were evenly divided into three age groups: students in junior high school, students in high school, and adults aged 19 to 39 years (1985, p. 133). Respondents were asked if "exposure to X-rated materials had made them want to try anything they saw" (1985, p. 140). Two-thirds of the males reported "wanting to try some of the behavior depicted" (1985, p. 140). Bryant reports that the desire to imitate what is seen in pornography "progressively increases as age of respondents *decreases*" (1985, p. 140; emphasis added). Among the junior high school students, 72% of the males reported that "they wanted to try some sexual experiment or sexual behavior that they had seen in their initial exposure to X-rated material" (1985, p. 140).

In trying to ascertain if imitation had occurred, the respondents were asked: "Did you actually experiment with or try any of the behaviors depicted [within a few days of seeing the materials]?" (1985, p. 140). A quarter of the males answered that they had. A number of adult men answered "no," but said that some years later they had experimented with the behaviors portrayed. However, only imitations within a few days of seeing the materials were counted (1985, p. 140). Male high school students were the most likely (31%) to report trying the behaviors portrayed (1985, p. 141). Unfortunately, no information is available on the behaviors imitated by these males. Imitating pornography is cause for concern only when the behavior imitated is violent or abusive, or when the behavior is not wanted by one or more of the participants. Despite the unavailability of this information, Bryant's study is valuable in showing how common it is for males to *want* to imitate what they see in pornography, and for revealing that many *do* imitate it within a few days of viewing it. Furthermore, given the degrading and often violent content of pornography, as well as the youthfulness and presumable susceptibility of many of the viewers, how likely is it that these males only imitated or wished to imitate the non-sexist, non-degrading, and non-violent sexual behavior?

Almost all the research on pornography to date has been conducted on men and women who were at least 18 years old. But as Malamuth points out, there is "a research basis for expecting that children would be more susceptible to the influences of mass media, including violent pornography if they are exposed to it" than adults (1985, p. 107). Bryant's telephone interviews show that very large numbers of children now have access to both hard-core and soft-core materials. For example:

• The average age at which male respondents saw their first issue of *Playboy* or a similar magazine was 11 years (1985, p. 135).

• All of the high school age males surveyed reported having read or looked at *Playboy*, *Playgirl*, or some other soft-core magazine (1985, p. 134).

• High school males reported having seen an average of 16.1 issues, and junior high school males said they had seen an average of 2.5 issues.

• In spite of being legally under age, junior high students reported having seen an average of 16.3 "unedited sexy R-rated films" (1985, p. 135). (Although R-rated movies are not usually considered pornographic, many of them meet my definition of pornography.)

• The average age of first exposure to sexually oriented R-rated films for all respondents was 12.5 years (1985, p. 135).

• Nearly 70% of the junior high students surveyed reported that they had seen their first R-rated film before they were 13 (1985, p. 135).

• The vast majority of all the respondents reported exposure to hard-core, X-rated, sexually explicit material (1985, p. 135). Furthermore, "a larger proportion of high school students had seen X-rated films than any other age group, including adults": 84%, with the average age of first exposure being 16 years, 11 months (1985, p. 136).

In a more recent anonymous survey of 247 Canadian junior high school students whose average age was 14 years, James Check and Kristin Maxwell (1992) report that 87% of the boys and 61% of the girls said they had viewed video-pornography. The average age at first exposure was just under 12 years.

> 33% of the boys versus only 2% of the girls reported watching pornography once a month or more often. As well, 29% of the boys versus 1% of the girls reported that pornography was the source that had provided them with the most useful information about sex (i.e., more than parents, school, friends, etc.). Finally, boys who were frequent consumers of pornography and/or reported learning a lot from pornography were also more likely to say that it was "OK" to hold a girl down and force her to have intercourse.

Clearly, more research is needed on the effects of pornography on young male viewers, particularly in view of the fact that recent studies suggest that "over 50% of various categories of paraphiliacs [sex offenders] had developed their deviant arousal patterns prior to age 18" (Einsiedel, 1986, p. 53). Einsiedel goes on to say that "it is clear that the age-of-first-exposure variable and the nature of that exposure needs to be examined more carefully. There is also evidence that the longer the duration of the paraphilia, the more significant the association with use of pornography" (Abel, Mittelman, and Becker, 1985).

The first two items listed under Factor I in my theoretical model both relate to the viewing of *violent* pornography. But sexualizing dominance and submission is a way in which non-violent pornography can also predispose some males to want to rape women.

(3) *Sexualizing dominance and submission*

Canadian psychologists James Check and Ted Guloien (1989) conducted an experiment in which they distinguished between degrading non-violent pornography and erotica, and compared their effects. Their experiment is rare not only for making this distinction, but also for including non-students as subjects; 436 Toronto residents and college students were exposed to one of three types of sexual material over three viewing sessions, or to no material. The sexual materials were constructed from existing commercially available videos and validated by measuring subjects' perceptions of them. The contents of the sexual materials shown to the three groups of subjects were as follows:

1. The *sexual violence* material portrayed scenes of sexual intercourse involving a woman strapped to a table and being penetrated by a large plastic penis.

2. The *sexually explicit,* dehumanizing but *non-violent* material portrayed scenes of sexual activity that included a man sitting on top of a woman and masturbating into her face.

3. The *sexually explicit non-degrading* material portrayed sexual activities leading up to heterosexual intercourse (Check and Guloien, 1989).

Check and Guloien's experiment revealed that the viewing of both the non-violent dehumanizing materials as well as the violent materials resulted in male subjects reporting a significantly greater likelihood of engaging in rape or other coercive sex acts than the control group.

Although self-reported likelihood of raping is not a proper measure of *desire* to rape, as it also indicates that the internal inhibitions against acting out rape desires have been undermined to some extent, Check and Guloien's experiment does offer tentative support for my theoretical model's claim that pornography sexualizes dominance and submission. In addition, it makes theoretical sense that sexualizing dominance and submission would probably be generalized to include eroticizing rape and/or other abusive sexual behavior for some males. For example, Ms. S testified at the Minnesota Hearings that: "Men constantly witness the abuse of women in pornography and if they can't engage in that behavior with their wives, girlfriends, or children, they force a whore to do it" (Russell, 1993a). And the Rev. Susan Wilhem testified in support of an anti-pornography ordinance in New York City that, "I came across a picture [in pornography] of a position my ex-husband had insisted we try. When we did, I hemorrhaged for three days. My bruised cervix is still a problem after ten years.... We should have some place to go to complain about how pornography is part of making our husbands into rapists" (Russell, 1993a).

Further research is needed on this issue, and more researchers need to follow the lead of the Canadian researchers in going beyond the distinction between violent and non-violent pornography, and distinguishing also between non-violent degrading pornography and erotica.

(4) Creating an appetite for increasingly stronger material

Dolf Zillmann and Jennings Bryant have studied the effects of what they refer to as "massive exposure" to pornography (1984). (In fact, it was not particularly massive: 4 hours and 48 minutes per week over a period of six weeks.) These researchers, unlike Malamuth and Donnerstein, focus on trying to ascertain the effects of *non-violent* pornography and, in the study to be described, they use a sample drawn from a non-student adult population.

Male subjects in the *massive exposure* condition saw 36 non-violent pornographic films, six per session per week; male subjects in the *intermediate* condition saw 18 such movies, three per session per week. Male subjects in the control group saw 36 non-pornographic movies. Various measures were taken after one week, two weeks, and three weeks of exposure, as well as information about the kind of materials that the subjects were most interested in viewing.

Zillmann and Bryant found that a desire for stronger material was fostered in their subjects. "Consumers graduate from common to less common forms of pornography," Zillmann maintains, that is, to more violent and more degrading materials (1984, p. 127). Zillmann suggests this may be "because familiar material becomes unexciting as a result of habituation" (1984, p. 127).

According to Zillmann and Bryant's research, then, pornography can transform a male who was not previously interested in the more abusive types of pornography, into one who *is* turned on by such material. This is consistent with Malamuth's findings (described on p. 124) that males who did not previously find rape sexually arousing, generate such fantasies after being exposed to a typical example of violent pornography.

II. THE ROLE OF PORNOGRAPHY IN UNDERMINING SOME MALES' INTERNAL INHIBITIONS AGAINST ACTING OUT THE DESIRE TO RAPE

"The movie was just like a big picture stand with words on it saying 'go out and do it, everybody's doin' it, even the movies.' " (Rapist interviewed by Beneke, 1982, p. 74.)

Evidence has been cited showing that many males would like to rape a woman, but that an unknown percentage of these males have internal inhibitions against doing so. Some males' internal inhibitions are likely to be very weak, others' very strong. Presumably, the strength of internal inhibitions also varies in the same individual from time to time. Seven ways in which pornography undermines some males' internal inhibitions against acting out rape desires are listed in Figure 1. Research evidence about these processes will be presented in this section.

(1) *Objectifying women.* The first way in which pornography undermines some males' internal inhibitions against acting out their desires to rape is by objectifying women. Feminists have been emphasizing the role of objectification in the occurrence of rape for years (e.g., Medea and Thompson, 1974; Russell, 1975). Objectification makes it easier to rape them. "It was difficult for me to admit that I was dealing with a human being when I was talking to a woman," one rapist reported, "because, if you read men's magazines, you hear about your stereo, your car, your chick" (Russell, 1975, pp. 249-250). After this rapist had hit his victim several times in her face, she stopped resisting and begged, "All right, just don't hurt me." "When she said that," he reported, "all of a sudden it came into my head, 'My God, this is a human being!' I came to my senses and saw that I was hurting this person." Another rapist said of his victim, "I wanted this beautiful fine *thing* and I got it" (Russell, 1975, p. 245, emphasis added).

Another example is provided by Ms. N who testified at the Hearings on Pornography in Minnesota about how her boyfriend treated her as a sexual object after he had watched pornography: "This encounter differed from previous ones. It was much quicker, it was somewhat rougher, and he was not aware of me as a person. There was no foreplay" (Russell, 1993a).

Dehumanizing oppressed groups or enemy nations in times of war is an important mechanism for facilitating brutal behavior toward members of those groups. Ms. U, for example, testified that: "A society that sells books, movies, and video games like 'Custer's Last Stand' ['Custer's Revenge'] in its street corners, gives white men permission to do what they did to me. Like they [her rapists] said, I'm scum. It is a game to track me down, rape and torture me" (Russell, 1993a). However, the dehumanization of women that occurs in pornography is often not recognized because of its sexual guise and its pervasiveness. It is important to note that the objectification of women is as common in non-violent pornography as it is in violent pornography.

Doug McKenzie-Mohr and Mark Zanna conducted an experiment to test whether certain types of males would be more likely to sexually objectify a woman after viewing 15 minutes of non-violent pornography. They selected 60 male students who they classified into one of two categories: masculine sex-typed or gender schematic — individuals who "encode all cross-sex interactions in sexual terms and all members of the opposite sex in terms of sexual attractiveness" (Bem, 1981, p. 361); and androgynous or gender aschematic — males who do not encode cross-sex interactions and women in these ways (McKenzie-Mohr and Zanna, 1990, p. 297, 299).

McKenzie-Mohr and Zanna found that after exposure to non-violent pornography, the masculine sex-typed males "treated our female experimenter who was interacting with them in a professional setting, in a manner that was both cognitively and behaviorally sexist" (1990, p. 305). In comparison with the androgynous males, for example, the masculine sex-typed males positioned themselves closer to the female experimenter and had "greater recall for information about her physical appearance" and less about the survey she was conducting (1990, p. 305). The experimenter also rated these males as more sexually motivated based on her answers to questions such as, "How much did you feel he was looking at your body?" "How sexually motivated did you find the subject?" (1990, p. 301).

This experiment confirmed McKenzie-Mohr and Zanna's hypothesis that exposure to non-violent pornography causes masculine sex-typed males, in contrast to androgynous males, to view and treat a woman as a sex object.

(2) *Rape myths.* If males believe that women enjoy rape and find it sexually exciting, this belief is likely to undermine the inhibitions of some of those who would like to rape women. Sociologists Diana Scully and Martha Burt have reported that rapists are particularly apt to believe rape myths (Burt, 1980; Scully, 1985). Scully, for example, found that 65% of the rapists in her study believed that "women cause their own rape by the way they act and the clothes they wear"; and 69% agreed that "most men accused of rape are really innocent." However, as Scully points out, it is not possible to know if their beliefs preceded their behavior or constitute

an attempt to rationalize it. Hence, findings from the experimental data are more telling for our purposes than these interviews with rapists.

As the myth that women enjoy rape is widely held, the argument that consumers of pornography realize that such portrayals are false, is totally unconvincing (Brownmiller, 1975; Burt, 1980; Russell, 1975). Indeed, several studies have shown that portrayals of women enjoying rape and other kinds of sexual violence can lead to increased acceptance of rape myths in both males and females. In an experiment conducted by Neil Malamuth and James Check, for example, one group of college students saw a pornographic depiction in which a woman was portrayed as sexually aroused by sexual violence, and a second group was exposed to control materials. Subsequently, all subjects were shown a second rape portrayal. The students who had been exposed to the pornographic depiction of rape were significantly more likely than the students in the control group (1) to perceive the second rape victim as suffering less trauma; (2) to believe that she actually enjoyed it; and (3) to believe that women in general enjoy rape and forced sexual acts (Check and Malamuth, 1985, p. 419).

Other examples of the rape myths that male subjects in these studies are more apt to believe after viewing pornography are as follows: "A woman who goes to the home or the apartment of a man on their first date implies that she is willing to have sex;" "Any healthy woman can successfully resist a rapist if she really wants to;" "Many women have an unconscious wish to be raped, and may then unconsciously set up a situation in which they are likely to be attacked;" "If a girl engages in necking or petting and she lets things get out of hand, it is her own fault if her partner forces sex on her" (Briere, Malamuth, and Check, 1985, p. 400).

In Maxwell and Check's 1992 study of 247 high school students (described on page 128), they found very high rates of what they called "rape supportive beliefs," that is, acceptance of rape myths and violence against women. The boys who were the most frequent consumers of pornography and/or who reported learning a lot from it, were more accepting of rape supportive beliefs than their peers who were less frequent consumers and/or who said they had not learned as much from it.

A full 25% of girls and 57% of boys indicated belief that in one or more situations, it was at least "maybe okay" for a boy to hold a girl down and force her to have intercourse. Further, only 21% of the boys and 57% of the girls believed that forced intercourse was "definitely not okay" in any of the situations. The situation in which forced intercourse was most accepted, was that in which the girl had sexually excited her date. In this case 43% of the boys and 16% of the girls stated that it was at least "maybe okay" for the boy to force intercourse (1992).

According to Donnerstein, "After only 10 minutes of exposure to aggressive pornography, particularly material in which women are shown being aggressed against, you find male subjects are much more willing to accept these particular myths" (1983, p. 6). These males are also more inclined to believe that 25% of the women they know would enjoy being raped (1983, p. 6).

(3) *Acceptance of interpersonal violence.* Males' internal inhibitions against acting out their desire to rape can also be undermined if they consider male violence against women to be acceptable behavior. Studies have shown that viewing portrayals of sexual violence as having positive consequences increases male subjects' acceptance of violence against women. Examples of some of the attitudes used to measure acceptance of interpersonal violence include "Being roughed up is sexually stimulating to many women;" "Sometimes the only way a man can get a cold woman turned on is to use force;" "Many times a woman will pretend she doesn't want to have intercourse because she doesn't want to seem loose, but she's really hoping the man will force her" (Briere, Malamuth, and Check, 1985, p. 401).

Malamuth and Check (1981) conducted an experiment of particular interest because the movies shown were part of the regular campus film program. Students were randomly assigned to view either a feature-length film that portrayed violence against women as being justifiable and having positive consequences (*Swept Away* or *The Getaway*) or a film without sexual violence. The experiment showed that exposure to the sexually violent movies increased the male subjects' acceptance of interpersonal violence against women. (This outcome did not occur with the female subjects.) These effects were measured several days after the films had been seen.

Malamuth suggests several processes by which sexual violence in the media "might lead to attitudes that are more accepting of violence against women" (1986, p. 4). Some of these processes also probably facilitate the undermining of pornography consumers' internal inhibitions against acting out rape desires.

1. Labelling sexual violence more as a sexual than a violent act.

2. Adding to perceptions that sexual aggression is normative and culturally acceptable.

3. Changing attributions of responsibility to place more blame on the victim.

4. Elevating the positive value of sexual aggression by associating it with sexual pleasure and a sense of conquest.

5. Reducing negative emotional reactions to sexually aggressive acts (1986, p. 5).

(4) *Trivializing rape.* According to Donnerstein, in most studies on the effects of pornography, "subjects have been exposed to only a few minutes of pornographic material" (1985, p. 341). In contrast, Zillmann and Bryant examined the impact on male subjects of what they refer to as "massive exposure" to non-violent pornography (4 hours and 48 minutes per week over a period of six weeks; for further details about the experimental design, see page 130). After three weeks the subjects were told that they were participating in an American Bar Association study that required them to evaluate a trial in which a man was prosecuted for the rape of a female hitchhiker. At the end of this mock trial various measures were taken of the subjects' opinions about the trial and about rape in general. For example, they were asked to recommend the prison term they thought most fair.

Zillmann and Bryant found that the male subjects who were exposed to the massive amounts of pornography considered rape a less serious crime than they did before they were exposed to it; they thought that prison sentences for rape should be shorter; and they perceived sexual aggression and abuse as causing less suffering for the victims, even in the case of an adult male having sexual intercourse with a 12-year-old girl (1984, p. 132). They concluded that "heavy exposure to common non-violent pornography trivialized rape as a criminal offense" (1984, p. 117).

(5) *Callous attitudes toward female sexuality.* In the same experiment on massive exposure, Zillmann and Bryant also reported that, "males' sexual callousness toward women was significantly enhanced" (1984, p. 117). Male subjects, for example, became increasingly accepting of statements such as "A woman doesn't mean 'no' until she slaps you"; "A man should find them, fool them, fuck them, and forget them"; and "If they are old enough to bleed, they are old enough to butcher." However, judging by these items, it is difficult to distinguish sexual callousness from a general hostility to women.

(6) *Acceptance of male dominance in intimate relationships.* A marked increase in males' acceptance of male dominance in intimate relationships was yet another result of massive exposure to pornography (Zillmann and Bryant, 1984, p. 121). The notion that women are, or ought to be, equal in intimate relationships was more likely to be abandoned by these male subjects (1984, p. 122). Finally, their support of the women's liberation movement also declined sharply (1984, p. 134).

These findings demonstrate that pornography increases the acceptability of sexism. As Van White points out, "by using pornography, by looking at other human beings as a lower form of life, they [the pornographers] are perpetuating the same kind of hatred that brings racism to society" (1984).

The greater trivializing of rape by males, the increase in their callous attitudes toward female sexuality, and their greater acceptance of male domination, are all likely to contribute to undermining some males' inhibitions against acting out their desires to rape.

For example, Ms. O testified about the ex-husband of a woman friend and next door neighbor: "When he looked at the magazines, he made hateful, obscene, violent remarks about women in general and about me. He told me that because I am female I am here to be used and abused by him, and that because he is a male he is the master and I am his slave" (Russell, 1993a).

(7) *Desensitizing males to rape.* In an experiment specifically designed to study desensitization, Linz, Donnerstein, and Penrod showed ten hours of R-rated or X-rated movies over a period of five days to male subjects (Donnerstein and Linz, 1985, p. 34A). Some students saw X-rated movies depicting sexual assault; others saw X-rated movies depicting only consenting sex; and a third group saw R-rated sexually violent movies — for example, *I Spit on Your Grave*, *Toolbox Murders*, and *Texas Chainsaw Massacre*. Donnerstein (1983) describes *Toolbox Murders* as follows: There is an erotic bathtub scene in which a woman massages herself. A beautiful song is played. Then a psychotic killer enters with a nail gun. The music stops. He chases the woman around the room, then shoots her through the stomach with the nail gun. She falls across a chair. The song comes back on as he puts the nail gun to her forehead and blows her brains out. According to Donnerstein, many young males become sexually aroused by this movie (1983, p. 10).

Donnerstein and Linz point out that, "It has always been suggested by critics of media violence research that only those who are *already* predisposed toward violence are influenced by exposure to media violence" (1985, p. 34F). These experimenters, however, actually preselected their subjects to ensure that they were not psychotic, hostile, or anxious.

Donnerstein and Linz described the impact of the R-rated movies on their subjects as follows:

> Initially, after the first day of viewing, the men rated themselves as significantly above the norm for depression, anxiety, and annoyance on a mood adjective checklist. After each subsequent day of viewing, these scores dropped until, on the fourth day of viewing, the males' levels of anxiety, depression, and annoyance were indistinguishable from base-line norms (1985, p. 34F).

By the fifth day, the subjects rated the movies as less graphic and less gory and estimated fewer violent or offensive scenes than after the first day of viewing. They also rated the films as significantly less debasing and degrading to women, more humorous, and more enjoyable, and re-ported a greater willingness to see this type of film again (1985, p. 34F). However, their sexual arousal by this material did *not* decrease over this five-day period (Donnerstein, 1983, p. 10).

On the last day, the subjects went to a law school where they saw a documentary re-enactment of a real rape trial. A control group of subjects who had never seen the films also participated in this part of the experi-ment. Subjects who had seen the R-rated movies: (1) rated the rape victim as significantly more worthless, (2) rated her injury as significantly less severe, and (3) assigned greater blame to her for being raped than did the subjects who had not seen the film. In contrast, these effects were not observed for the X-rated non-violent films.[4] However, the results were much the same for the violent X-rated films, despite the fact that the R-rated material was "much more graphically violent" (Donnerstein, 1985, pp. 12-13).

In summary: I have presented only a small portion of the research

---

4   It is a mystery why Donnerstein finds no effects for non-violent pornographic movies while Zillmann reports many significant effects. Unfortunately, there is reason to believe that Donnerstein's reporting of his findings that have become unpopular in academia and other segments of the liberal establishment is not entirely accurate. For example, see Page, 1989, 1990a, 1990b; and Russell, "The experts cop out," in Russell, 1993b.

evidence for seven different effects of pornography, all of which probably contribute to the undermining of some males' internal inhibitions against acting out rape desires. This list is not intended to be comprehensive.

III. THE ROLE OF PORNOGRAPHY IN UNDERMINING SOME MALES' SOCIAL INHIBITIONS AGAINST ACTING OUT THEIR DESIRE TO RAPE.

"I have often thought about it [rape], fantasized about it. I might like it because of having a feeling of power over a woman. But I never actually wanted to through *fear of being caught and publicly ruined"* (Male respondent, Hite, 1981, p. 715, emphasis added).

A man may want to rape a woman *and* his internal inhibitions against rape may be undermined by his hostility to women or by his belief in the myths that women really enjoy being raped and/or that they deserve it, but he may still not act out his desire to rape because of his *social* inhibitions. Fear of being caught and convicted for the crime is the most obvious example of a social inhibition. In addition to Hite's respondent quoted above, a second man's answer to her question on whether he had ever wanted to rape a woman illustrates this form of inhibition:

I have never raped a woman, but have at times felt a desire to — for the struggle and final victory. I'm a person, though, who always thinks before he acts, and *the consequences wouldn't be worth it. Besides I don't want to be known as a pervert* (1981, p. 715, emphasis added).

(1) *Diminishing fear of social sanctions.* In one of his early experiments, Malamuth, along with his colleagues, Haber and Feshbach (1980), reported that after reading the account of a violent rape by a stranger, 17% of their male student subjects admitted that there was some likelihood that they might behave in a similar fashion in the same circumstances. However, 53% of the same male students said there was some likelihood that they might act as the rapist did *if they could be sure of getting away with it.* The 36% difference in these percentages reveals the significant role that can be played by social inhibitions against acting out rape desires. My hypothesis is that pornography also plays a role in undermining some males' social inhibitions against acting out their desire to rape.

In his content analysis of 150 pornographic home videos, Palys investigated "whether aggressive perpetrators ever received any negative consequences for their aggressive activity — if charges were laid, or the person felt personal trauma, or had some form of 'just deserts' " (1986, p.

32). The answer was no in 73% of the cases in which a clear-cut answer was ascertainable. Similarly, Don Smith (1976) found that fewer than 3% of the rapists portrayed in the 428 pornographic books he analyzed were depicted as experiencing any negative consequences as a result of their behavior. Indeed, many of them were rewarded. The common portrayal in pornography of rape as easy to get away with probably contributes to the undermining of some males' social inhibitions against the acting out of their rape desires.

If there were more effective social sanctions against pornography, this would almost certainly increase the reluctance of some people to participate in the pornography industry. There are many reasons why progressive people are strenuously opposed to government efforts to censor pornography. There are, however, many alternative kinds of sanctions that need to be explored. For example, many women have been forced to participate in pornography against their will. I would have thought that pornographic publications that publish photos of these women would be accessories after-the-fact to false imprisonment, rape, assault, and sometimes, possibly, murder.

(2) *Diminishing fear of disapproval by peers.* Fear of disapproval from one's peers is another social inhibition that may be undermined by pornography. Zillmann, for example, found that "massive" exposure to non-violent pornography caused subjects to overestimate the number of people who engage in uncommon sexual practices, such as anal intercourse, group sexual activities, sadomasochism, and bestiality (1985, p. 118). Rape is portrayed as a very common male practice in much violent pornography, and the actors themselves may serve as a kind of pseudo-peer group and/or role models for consumers. Further research is needed to evaluate these hypotheses.

In general, I hypothesize the following disinhibiting effects of viewing violent pornography, particularly in "massive" amounts: (a) viewers' estimates of the percentage of other males who have raped women would probably increase; (b) viewers would be likely to consider rape a much easier crime to commit than they had previously believed; (c) viewers would be less likely to believe that rape survivors would report their rapes to the police; (d) viewers would be more likely to expect that rapists would avoid arrest, prosecution and conviction in those cases that are reported; (e) viewers would become less disapproving of rapists, and less likely to expect disapproval from others if they decided to rape.

IV. THE ROLE OF PORNOGRAPHY IN UNDERMINING POTENTIAL VICTIMS' ABILITIES TO AVOID OR RESIST RAPE

"He...told me it was not wrong because they were doing it in the magazines and that made it O.K." (*Attorney General's Commission*, 1986, p. 786).

Obviously, this fourth factor (the role of pornography in undermining potential victim's abilities to avoid or resist rape) is not necessary for rape to occur. Nevertheless, once the first three factors in my causal model have been met — a male not only wants to rape a woman but is willing to do so because his inhibitions, both internal and social, have been undermined — a would-be rapist may use pornography to try to undermine a woman's resistance. Pornography is more likely to be used for this purpose when males attack their intimates (as opposed to strangers).

(1) *Encouraging females to get into high rape-risk situations.* Most adult rape victims are not shown pornography in the course of being raped, although the testimony of prostitutes reveals that this is quite a common experience for many of them who are raped (*Everywoman*, 1988; Russell, 1993a). But pornography is more often used to try to persuade a woman or child to engage in certain acts, to legitimize the acts, and to undermine their resistance, refusal, or disclosure of these acts. Donald Mosher, for example, reported in his 1971 study that 16% of the "sex calloused" male students had attempted to obtain intercourse by showing pornography to a woman, or by taking her to a "sexy" movie. When this strategy succeeds in manipulating women into so-called sex play, it can make women very vulnerable to date rape.

In a more recent study conducted in Canada, Charlene Senn found that "the more pornography women were exposed to, the more likely they were to have been forced or coerced into sexual activity they did not want" (1992). In addition, a male was present in most of the cases in which women were exposed to pornography. This suggests that most women who consume pornography do so because a man wants them to (1992). This is a particularly important finding because the media have made much of the alleged fact that increasing numbers of women are renting pornographic videos, presuming that they do so for their own gratification.

There are at least two possible explanations for the positive correlation between the quantity of pornography to which women are exposed and their experiences of forced or coerced sex. It could be that women who co-operate with males' requests to view pornography are more likely to be sexually assaulted because viewing pornography somehow undermines their ability to avoid being sexually assaulted. Or perhaps women who can be coerced into viewing pornography can also more easily be coerced sexually than women who refuse to view it.

Ms. M describes how her husband's continual pornography-related abuse of her during their years together almost drove her to suicide:

> I could see how I was being seasoned by the use of pornography and I could see what would come next. I could see more violence and I could see more humiliation, and I knew at that point I was either going to die from it — I would kill myself — or I would leave. And I felt strong enough to leave (Russell, 1993a).

When women are shown such materials, they probably feel more obliged to engage in unwanted sex acts that they mistakenly believe are normal. The Reverend Susan Wilhem, for example, testified about her ex-husband that pornography "made him expect that I would want to do crazy things" (Russell, 1993a). Evidence for this hypothesis is provided by Zillmann and Bryant's previously mentioned findings that massive exposure to pornography distorts the viewers' perceptions of sexuality by producing the lasting impression that relatively uncommon sexual practices are more common than they actually are; for example, "intercourse with more than one partner at a time, sadomasochistic actions, and animal contacts" (1984, pp. 132-133).

The following statements by two other women reveal how their husbands used pornography for this purpose.

> Once we saw an X-rated film that showed anal intercourse. After that he insisted that I try anal intercourse. I agreed to do so, trying to be the available, willing creature that I thought I was supposed to be. I found the experience very painful, and I told him so. But he kept insisting that we try it again and again (*Attorney General's Commission*, 1986, p. 778).

> He told me that if I loved him I would do these things, and that, as I could see from the things that he had read to me in the magazines, a lot of times women didn't like it initially, but if I tried it enough, I would probably like it or learn to like it. Then he read me stories where women learned to like it (Russell, 1993a).

More systematic research is needed to establish how frequently males use pornography to try to undermine women's ability to avoid or resist rape and other sexual abuse, and how effective this strategy is.

(2) *A pornography industry that requires female participation.* Because the portrayal of rape is one of the favorite themes of pornography, a large and ever-changing supply of girls and women have to be found to provide it. Clearly, some women are voluntary participants in simulated acts of rape. But many of the rapes that are photographed are real (for examples, see *Everywoman*, 1988; Russell, 1993a).

In summary: A significant amount of research supports my theory that pornography can, and does, cause rape. Nevertheless, much of the research undertaken to date does not adequately examine the four key variables in my theory. Malamuth's concept of males' self-reported likelihood to rape women, for example, merges the notion of a *desire* to rape with my notion that internal inhibitions against acting out this desire can be undermined. So if a man says that there is some likelihood that he would rape a woman if he could get away with it, he is saying both that he has the desire to rape a woman *and* that his internal inhibitions against doing so are at least somewhat undermined (the degree of undermining depends on whether he is very likely, somewhat likely, or only slightly likely to do it). I hope that more research will be guided in the future by the theoretical distinctions required by my model.

FURTHER EMPIRICAL FINDINGS ON THE CAUSATIVE ROLE OF PORNOGRAPHY IN RAPE

The 25% to 30% of male students who admit that there is some likelihood that they would rape a woman if they could be assured of getting away with it, increases to 57% after exposure to sexually violent images, particularly sexually violent images depicting women enjoying rape (Donnerstein, 1983, p. 7). This means that *as a result of one brief exposure to pornography, the number of males who are willing to consider rape as a plausible act for them to commit actually doubles.*

One such brief exposure to pornography also increases male subjects' acceptance of rape myths and interpersonal violence against women. Given the hypothesis that such increased acceptance would serve to lower viewers' inhibitions against acting out violent desires, one would expect pornography consumption to be related to rape rates. This is what the following ingenious study found.

Larry Baron and Murray Straus (1984) undertook a 50-state correlational analysis of reported rape rates and the circulation rates of eight pornographic magazines: *Chic, Club, Forum, Gallery, Genesis, Hustler, Oui,* and *Playboy.* A highly significant correlation (+0.64) was found between reported rape rates and circulation rates. Baron and Straus attempted to ascertain what other factors might possibly explain this correlation. Their statistical analysis revealed that the proliferation of pornographic magazines and the level of urbanization explained more of the variance in rape rates than the other variables investigated (for example, social disorganization, economic inequality, unemployment, sexual inequality).

In another important study, Mary Koss conducted a large national survey of over 6,000 college students selected by a probability sample of institutions of higher education (Koss, Gidycz, and Wisniewski, 1987). She found that college males who reported behavior that meets common legal definitions of rape were significantly more likely than college males who denied such behavior to be frequent readers of at least one of the following magazines: *Playboy, Penthouse, Chic, Club, Forum, Gallery, Genesis, Oui,* or *Hustler* (Koss and Dinero, 1989).

Several other studies have assessed the correlation between the degree of males' exposure to pornography and attitudes supportive of violence against women. Malamuth reports that in three out of four studies, "higher levels of reported exposure to sexually explicit media correlated with higher levels of attitudes supportive of violence against women" (1986, p. 8).

(1) Malamuth and Check (1985) conducted a study in which they found a positive correlation between the amount of sexually explicit magazines a sample of college males read and their beliefs that women enjoy forced sex.

(2) Similarly, Check (1985) found that the more often a diverse sample of Canadian males were exposed to pornography, the higher their acceptance of rape myths, violence against women, and general sexual callousness was.

(3) Briere, Corne, Runtz and Malamuth (1984) found similar correlations in another sample of college males.

In her study of male sexuality, Shere Hite found that 67% of the males who admitted that they had wanted to rape a woman reported reading pornographic magazines, compared to only 19% of those who said that they had never wanted to rape a woman (1981, p. 1123). With regard to the frequency of exposure to pornography, Hite reported that only 11% of the 7,000 males she surveyed said that they had never looked at pornography; 36% said they viewed it regularly, 21% said they did so sometimes, 26% said they did so infrequently, and 6% said that they had looked at it in the past (1981, p. 1123). While correlation does not prove causation, and it therefore cannot be concluded from these studies that it was the consumption of the pornography that was responsible for the males' higher acceptance of violence against women, their findings are consistent with a theory that a causal connection exists.

If the rape rate was very low in the United States, or if it had declined over the past few decades, such findings would probably be cited to support the view that pornography does not play a causative role in rape. While drawing such a conclusion would not be warranted, it is nevertheless of interest to note that my probability sample survey in San Francisco shows that a dramatic increase in the rape rate has occurred in the United States over the last several decades, during which there has also been a great proliferation of pornography (Russell, 1984). Unlike the rapes studied by Straus and Baron, 90% of the rapes and attempted rapes described in my survey were never reported to the police.

With regard to experimental work, Donnerstein points out that, "one cannot, for obvious reasons, experimentally examine the relationship between pornography and *actual* sexual aggression" (1984, p. 53). He has, however, conducted experiments that show that the level of aggression of male subjects toward females increases after they have been exposed to violent pornography in which a female rape victim was portrayed as becoming aroused by the end of the movie. (Aggression was measured by the intensity of electric shock subjects were willing to administer.) Violent films that were non-pornographic (depicting, for example, a man hitting a woman) also increased male subjects' levels of aggression toward women, but not to the same extent as violent pornographic films. When Donnerstein used violent pornography in which the victim was portrayed as being distressed by the sexual assault throughout the movie, the levels of aggression of male subjects toward females became increased only when they had first been angered by a confederate of the experimenter before seeing the movie.

To explain why male subjects' aggression toward women increases the most after seeing pornography that depicts a female rape victim becoming sexually aroused by the assault, Malamuth suggested that: "positive victim reactions...may act to justify aggression and to reduce general inhibitions against aggression" (1984, p. 36). This interpretation is consistent with my causal model's emphasis on the important role pornographic depictions play in undermining males' inhibitions against acting out hostile behavior toward women.

Many psychologists reject the use of attitudes as a basis for predicting behavior. Similarly, some people question whether Malamuth's measure of males' self-reported likelihood to rape has any meaningful relationship with their rape behavior. Hence, Malamuth's experiment to test whether males' attitudes and sexual arousal to depictions of rape can predict non-sexual aggression in the laboratory is of particular interest. A week after measuring male subjects' attitudes and sexual arousal to rape, they were angered by a female confederate of the experimenter. When the subjects were given an opportunity to behave aggressively toward her by administering an unpleasant noise as punishment for errors she made in an alleged extrasensory perception experiment, males who had higher levels of sexual arousal to rape and who had attitudes that condoned aggression "were more aggressive against the woman and wanted to hurt her to a greater extent" (Malamuth, 1986, p. 16). On the basis of this experiment, as well as two others, Malamuth concluded finding that "attitudes condoning aggression against women related to objectively observable behavior — laboratory aggression against women" (1986, p. 16).

Both Donnerstein and Malamuth emphasize that their findings on the relationship between pornography and aggression toward women relate to aggressive or violent, not to non-violent, pornography. Donnerstein, for example, maintains that "nonaggressive materials only affect aggression when inhibitions to aggress are quite low, or with long-term and massive exposure. With a single exposure and normal aggressing conditions, there is little evidence that nonviolent pornography has any negative effects" (1984, pp. 78-79). In the real world, however, inhibitions on aggressive behavior are often very low, and long-term and massive exposure to non-violent material is also quite common. Furthermore, there is a lot of evidence of harm from non-aggressive pornography, aside from its impact on aggressive behavior (for example, see my earlier discussion of some of Zillmann's findings).

Finally, given how saturated United States culture is with pornographic images and how much exposure many of the male subjects being tested have already had, the task of trying to design experiments that can show effects on the basis of one more exposure is challenging indeed. When no measurable effects result, it would be wrong, because of this methodological problem, to interpret the experiment as proving that there are no effects in general. We should focus, therefore, on the effects that *do* show up, rather than being overly impressed by the effects that do not.

Some people are critical of the fact that most of the experimental research on pornography has been conducted on college students who are not representative of males in the general population. Hence, the research of Richard Frost and John Stauffer (1987) comparing the responses to filmed violence of college students and residents of an inner-city housing project is of particular interest.

In five of the ten violent films shown to these two groups the violence was directed at females. Frost and Stauffer evaluated these male's sexual arousal to these films by applying both self-report and physiological measures. They found that "there was no single form of violence for which the responses of the college sample exceeded those of the inner city sample on either measure" (1987, p. 36). Four of the five most physiologically arousing categories of violence were the same for both groups: a female killing another female; a male killing a female; rape/murder; and a female killing a male (1987, p. 37). Interestingly, depictions of male/female assault were the least exciting to all subjects of all ten types of violence measured (1987, p. 39).

The greatest disparity between the two groups in both physiological and self-reported sexual arousal was to depictions of rape. These "caused the highest response by inner-city subjects but only the fifth highest by the college sample" (1987, p. 38). Although it is not acceptable to infer action from arousal, nevertheless there is evidence that males who are aroused by depictions of violence toward women are more likely to act violently toward them than males who are not aroused by such depictions.

Hence, Frost and Stauffer's study suggests that college students are less prone to sexual violence than some other groups of males. This will come as no surprise to many people, as inner-city environments are more violent than colleges or than the places in which most college students grew up. One reason this finding is significant is that most of the research in this area has been conducted on college males. It is important to realize that the high percentages of male college students who admit that they might rape women, for example, might well be even higher if samples were drawn from non-student populations.

The exposure of sex offenders to pornography is another area of research that is relevant to the causal connections between pornography and rape. It is well known that many sex offenders claim that viewing pornography affects their criminal behavior. Ted Bundy is perhaps the most notorious of these males. For example, in one study of 89 non-incarcerated sex offenders conducted by William Marshall, "slightly more than one-third of the child molesters and rapists reported at least occasionally being incited to commit an offense by exposure to forced or consenting pornography" (Einsiedel, 1986, p. 62). Exactly a third of the rapists who reported being incited by pornography to commit an offense said that they deliberately used pornography in their preparation for committing the rape. The comparable figure for child molesters was much higher — 53% versus 33% (Einsiedel, 1986, p. 62).

However, as these sex offenders appear to have used the pornography to arouse themselves after they had already decided to commit an offense, it could be argued that it was not the pornography that incited them. To what extent they actually required the pornography in order to commit their offenses, like some perpetrators require alcohol, we do not know. Even if these perpetrators were eliminated from the data analysis, however, that still leaves 66% of the rapists and 47% of the child molesters who claimed that they were at least sometimes incited by pornography to commit an offense.

Gene Abel, Mary Mittelman, and Judith Becker (1985) evaluated the use of pornography by 256 perpetrators of sexual offenses, all of whom were undergoing assessment and treatment. Like Marshall's sample, these males were outpatients, not incarcerated offenders. This is important because there is evidence that the data provided by incarcerated and non-incarcerated offenders differ (Einsiedel, 1986, p. 47). Abel and his colleagues reported that 56% of the rapists and 42% of the child molesters implicated pornography in the commission of their offenses. Edna Einsiedel, in her review of the social science research for the 1985 Attorney General's Commission of Pornography, concluded that these studies "are suggestive of the implication of pornography in the commission of sex crimes among *some* rapists and child molesters" (p. 63, emphasis in original).

In another study, Michael Goldstein and Harold Kant found that incarcerated rapists had been exposed to hard-core pornography at an earlier age than males presumed to be non-rapists. Specifically, 30% of the rapists in their sexual offender sample said that they had encountered hard-core pornographic photos in their preadolescence (i.e., before the age of 11; 1973, p. 55). This 30% figure compares with only 2% of the control group subjects exposed to hard-core pornography as preadolescents. (The control group was obtained by a random household sample that was matched with the offender group for age, race, religion, and educational level; 1973, p. 50). Could it be that this early exposure of the offenders to hard-core pornography played a role in making them rapists? Hopefully, future research will address this question.

CONCLUSION

In Part 2 of this book, I have described my theory that pornography — both violent and non-violent — can cause rape, citing the findings of recent research that support this theory. I believe that my theory can be adapted to apply to other forms of sexual assault and abuse, as well as to woman battering and femicide (the misogyny-motivated killing of women). I have done the preliminary work on such an adaptation to the causal relationship between pornography and child sexual abuse and plan to publish this work in the future.

In conclusion, I believe that the rich and varied data now available to us from all kinds of sources, when considered together, strongly support my theory.

• A high percentage of non-incarcerated rapists and child molesters have said that they have been incited by pornography to commit crimes;

• Pre-selected normal healthy male students say they are more likely to rape a woman after just one exposure to violent pornography;

• A high percentage of male junior high school students, high school students, and adults in a non-laboratory survey report imitating X-rated movies within a few days of exposure;

• Hundreds of women have testified in public about how they have been victimized by pornography;

• Ten percent of a probability sample of 930 women in San Francisco and 25% of female subjects in an experiment on pornography in Canada reported having been upset by requests to enact pornography (Russell, 1980, and Senn and Radtke, 1986);

• Many prostitutes report that they have experienced pornography-related sexual assault (Silbert and Pines, 1984; Everywoman, 1988; and Russell, 1993a);

• The laws of social learning must surely apply to pornography at least as much as to the mass media in general. Indeed, I — and others —

have argued that sexual arousal and orgasm are likely to serve as unusually potent reinforcers of the messages conveyed by pornography;

- A large body of experimental research has shown that the viewing of violent pornography results in higher rates of aggression against women by male subjects.

It is no wonder that Donnerstein stated that the relationship between pornography and violence against women is stronger than the relationship between smoking and lung cancer (see epigraph at beginning of Part 2). One of the effects of viewing non-violent pornography discovered by Zillmann is that "the more extensive the exposure, the more accepting of pornography subjects became" (Zillmann and Bryant, 1984, p. 133). Although females expressed significantly less acceptance than males, this effect also applied to females. Pornography has expanded into a multi-billion-dollar-a-year industry, and I believe we are seeing on a massive scale some of the very effects so brilliantly and carefully documented in some of the experiments by Malamuth, Donnerstein, Zillmann, and their colleagues. Donnerstein's description of the desensitization that occurred in healthy pre-selected male students after only five days of viewing woman-slashing films may apply to ever-growing segments of our society (Donnerstein, Linz and Penrod, 1987).

Van White, the Chairperson of the Hearings on Pornography in Minnesota in 1983, commented as follows on the impact of the testimony by the survivors of pornography-related abuse: "These horror stories made me think of the history of slavery in this country—how Black women were at the bottom of the pile, treated like animals instead of human beings. As I listened to these victims of pornography, I heard young women describe how they felt about…the way women's breasts and genitals are displayed and women's bodies are shown in compromising postures. I thought about the time of slavery, when Black women had their bodies invaded, their teeth and limbs examined, their bodies checked out for breeding, checked out as you would an animal, and I said to myself, 'We've come a long way, haven't we?'

"Today we have an industry…showing women in the same kind of submissive and animalistic roles" (1984).

United States' culture appears to have been affected by the very effects the research shows. The massive propaganda campaign is working; people now actually *see* differently. Pornography has to become increasingly extreme before people are disturbed by, or even notice, the violence and degradation portrayed in it. Very few see the real abuse that is happening to some of the women who are photographed. As Zillmann and Bryant show, "heavy consumption of common forms of pornography fosters an appetite for stronger materials" (1984, p. 127). What was considered hard-core in the past has become soft-core in the present. Where will this all end? Will we as a culture forever refuse to read the writing on the wall?

These are some of the women activists in the rampage against *Penthouse* for its publication of the photo essay on Asian women in the December 1984 issue (see examples on pages 102-105), demanding a boycott of some of the businesses that advertise in this pornographic magazine. (Photo courtesy of Melissa Farley.)

REFERENCES

Abel, Gene; Barlow, David; Blanchard, Edward, and Guild, Donald. (1977). The components of rapists' sexual arousal. *Archives of General Psychiatry, 34,* 895-903.

Abel, Gene; Mittelman, Mary, and Becker, Judith. (1985). Sexual offenders: Results of assessment and recommendations for treatment. In Mark Ben-Aron, Stephen Hucker, and Christopher Webster (Eds.), *Clinical Criminology: The Assessment and Treatment of Criminal Behavior* (pp. 191-205). Toronto: Clarke Institute of Psychiatry, University of Toronto.

Attorney General's Commission on Pornography: Final Report. (1986). (Vols. I-II). Washington, DC: U.S. Department of Justice.

Baron, Larry and Straus, Murray. (1984). Sexual stratification, pornography, and rape in the United States. In Neil Malamuth and Edward Donnerstein (Eds.), *Pornography and Sexual Aggression* (pp. 185-209). New York: Academic Press.

Bart, Pauline, and Jozsa, Margaret. (1980). Dirty books, dirty film, and dirty data. In Laura Lederer (Ed.), *Take Back the Night: Women on Pornography* (pp. 204-217). New York: William Morrow.

Bem, Sandra. (1991). Gender schema theory: A cognitive account of sex typing. *Psychological Review, 88,* 354-364.

Beneke, Timothy. (1982). *Men on Rape.* New York: St. Martin's Press.

Bogdanovich, Peter. (1984). *The Killing of the Unicorn: Dorothy Stratten 1960-1980.* New York: William Morrow.

Briere, John; Corne, Shawn; Runtz, Marsha, and Malamuth, Neil. (1984). The rape arousal inventory: Predicting actual and potential sexual aggression in a university population. Paper presented at the American Psychological Association Meeting, Toronto.

Briere, John, and Malamuth, Neil. (1983). Self-reported likelihood of sexually aggressive behavior: Attitudinal versus sexual explanations. *Journal of Research in Personality, 17,* 315-323.

Briere, John; Malamuth, Neil, and Check, James. (1985). Sexuality and rape-supportive beliefs. *International Journal of Women's Studies, 8,* 398-403.

Brownmiller, Susan. (1975). *Against Our Will: Men, Women and Rape.* New York: Simon and Schuster.

Bryant, Jennings. (1985). Unpublished transcript of testimony to the Attorney General's Commission on Pornography Hearings, Houston, TX, pp. 128-157.

Burt, Martha. (1980). Cultural myths and supports for rape. *Journal of Personality and Social Psychology, 38*(2), 217-230.

Check, James. (1985). The effects of violent and non-violent pornography. Ottawa: Department of Justice, Canada.

Check, James, and Guloien, Ted. (1989). Reported proclivity for coercive sex following repeated exposure to sexually violent pornography, non-violent dehumanizing pornography, and erotica. In Dolf Zillmann and Jennings Bryant (Eds.), *Pornography: Recent Research, Interpretations, and Policy Considerations* (pp. 159-184). Hillside, NJ: Lawrence Erlbaum.

Check, James, and Malamuth, Neil. (1985). An empirical assessment of some feminist hypotheses about rape. *International Journal of Women's Studies, 8,* 414-423.

Check, James, and Malamuth, Neil. (1984). Can there be positive effects of participation in pornography experiments? *The Journal of Sex Research, 20*(1), 14-31.

Check, James, and Maxwell, Kristin. (1992, June). Children's consumption of pornography and their attitudes regarding sexual violence. Paper presented at the Canadian Psychological Association Meetings, Quebec. (Abstract)

Cline, Victor (Ed.). (1974). *Where Do You Draw the Line?* Provo, UT: Brigham Young University Press.

Diamond, Irene. (1980). Pornography and repression. In Laura Lederer (Ed.), *Take Back the Night: Women on Pornography* (pp. 187-203). New York: William Morrow.

Dietz, Park, and Evans, Barbara. (1982). Pornographic imagery and prevalence of paraphilia. *American Journal of Psychiatry, 139,* 1493-1495.

Donnerstein, Edward. (1983). Unpublished transcript of testimony to the Public Hearings on Ordinances to Add Pornography as Discrimination against Women. Committee on Government Operations, City Council, Minneapolis, MN, pp. 4-12.

Donnerstein, Edward. (1984). Pornography: Its effects on violence against women. In Neil Malamuth and Edward Donnerstein (Eds.), *Pornography and Sexual Aggression* (pp. 53-84). New York: Academic Press.

Donnerstein, Edward. (1985). Unpublished transcript of testimony to the Attorney General's Commission on Pornography Hearings, Houston, TX, pp. 5-33.

Donnerstein, Edward, and Linz, Daniel. (1985). Presentation paper to the Attorney General's Commission on Pornography, Houston, TX.

Donnerstein, Edward; Linz, Daniel, and Penrod, Steven. (1987). *The Question of Pornography: Research Findings and Policy Implications.* New York: Free Press.

Dworkin, Andrea, and MacKinnon, Catharine. (1988). Pornography and Civil Rights. Minneapolis, MN: Organizing Against Pornography.

Everywoman. (1988). *Pornography and Sexual Violence: Evidence of the Links.* London: Everywoman.

Finkelhor, David. (1984). *Child Sexual Abuse: New Theory and Research.* New York: Free Press.

Frost, Richard, and Stauffer, John. (1987, Spring). The effects of social class, gender, and personality on physiological responses to filmed violence. *Journal of Communication, 37*(2), 29-45.

Goldstein, Michael, and Kant, Harold. (1973). *Pornography and Sexual Deviance.* Berkeley, CA: University of California Press.

Goodchilds, Jacqueline, and Zellman, Gail. (1984). Sexual signalling and sexual aggression in adolescent relationships. In Neil Malamuth and Edward Donnerstein (Eds.), *Pornography and Sexual Aggression* (pp. 233-246). New York: Academic Press.

Hite, Shere. (1981). *The Hite Report on Male Sexuality*. New York: Alfred Knopf.

Itzin, Catherine (Ed.). (1992). *Pornography: Women, Violence and Civil Liberties*. London and New York: Oxford University Press.

Jacobs, Karen. (1984). Patterns of violence: A feminist perspective on the regulations of pornography. *The Harvard Women's Law Journal, 7,* 5-55.

Koss, Mary, and Dinero, Thomas. (1988). Predictors of sexual aggression among a national sample of male college students. In Vernon Quinsey and Robert Prentky (Eds.), *Human Sexual Aggression: Current Perspectives, Annals of the New York Academy of Sciences, 528,* 133-147.

Koss, Mary; Gidycz, Christine, and Wisniewski, Nadine. (1987). The scope of rape: Incidence and prevalence of sexual aggression and victimization in a national sample of higher education students. *Journal of Consulting and Clinical Psychology, 55,* 162-170.

Lederer, Laura (Ed.). (1980). *Take Back the Night: Women on Pornography*. New York: William Morrow.

Longino, Helen. (1980). What is pornography? In Laura Lederer (Ed.), *Take Back the Night* (pp. 40-54). New York: William Morrow.

Lovelace, Linda. (1981). *Ordeal*. New York: Berkeley Books.

Lovelace, Linda. (1986). *Out of Bondage*. Secaucus, NJ: Lyle Stuart.

MacKinnon, Catharine. (1987). *Feminism Unmodified: Discourses on Life and Law*. Cambridge, MA: Harvard University Press.

Malamuth, Neil. (1981a). Rape fantasies as a function of exposure to violent sexual stimuli. *Archives of Sexual Behavior, 10,* 33-47.

Malamuth, Neil. (1981b). Rape proclivity among males. *Journal of Social Issues, 37*(4), 138-157.

Malamuth, Neil. (1984). Aggression against women: Cultural and individual causes. In Neil Malamuth and Edward Donnerstein (Eds.), *Por-*

nography and Sexual Aggression (pp. 19-52). New York: Academic Press.

Malamuth, Neil. (1985). Unpublished transcript of testimony to the Attorney General's Commission on Pornography Hearings, Houston, TX, pp. 68-110.

Malamuth, Neil. (1986). Do sexually violent media indirectly contribute to anti-social behavior? Paper prepared for the Surgeon General's Workshop on Pornography and Public Health, Arlington, VA.

Malamuth, Neil, and Check, James. (1981). The effects of mass media exposure on acceptance of violence against women: A field experiment. *Journal of Research in Personality, 15,* 436-446.

Malamuth, Neil, and Check, James. (1985). The effects of aggressive pornography on beliefs in rape myths: Individual differences. *Journal of Research in Personality, 19,* 299-320.

Malamuth, Neil, and Donnerstein, Edward (Eds.). (1984). *Pornography and Sexual Aggression.* New York: Academic Press.

Malamuth, Neil; Haber, Scott, and Feshbach, Seymour. (1980). Testing hypotheses regarding rape: Exposure to sexual violence, sex differences, and the "normality" of rapists. *Journal of Research in Personality, 14,* 121-137.

Malamuth, Neil, and Spinner, Barry. (1980). A longitudinal content analysis of sexual violence in the best-selling erotic magazines. *Journal of Sex Research, 16*(3), 226-237.

Maxwell, Kristin, and Check, James. (1992, June). Adolescents' rape myth attitudes and acceptance of forced sexual intercourse. Paper presented at the Canadian Psychological Association Meetings, Quebec. (Abstract)

Mayall, Alice, and Russell, Diana. (1993). Racism in pornography. In Diana Russell (Ed.), *Making Violence Sexy: Feminist Views on Pornography,* New York: Teachers College Press.

McKenzie-Mohr, Doug, and Zanna, Mark. (1990). Treating women as sexual objects: Look to the (gender schematic) male who has viewed pornography. *Personality and Social Psychology Bulletin, 16*(2), 296-308.

Medea, Andra, and Thompson, Kathleen. (1974). *Against Rape.* New York: Farrar, Straus and Giroux.

Mosher, Donald. (1971). Sex callousness toward women. *Technical Reports of the Commission on Obscenity and Pornography, 8.* Washington, DC: U.S. Government Printing Office.

National Research Bureau Inc. (1992). *Working Press of the Nation: Magazine and Editorial Directory,* Vol. II, Burlington: Iowa.

Page, Stewart. (1989). Misrepresentation of pornography research: Psychology's role. *American Psychologist, 42*(10), 578-580.

Page, Stewart. (1990a). The turnaround on pornography research: Some implications for psychology and women. *Canadian Psychology, 31*(4), 359-367.

Page, Stewart. (1990b). On Lintz and Donnerstein's view of pornography research. *Canadian Psychology, 31*(4), 371-373.

Palys, T. (1986). Testing the common wisdom: The social content of video pornography. *Canadian Psychology, 27*(1), 22-35.

Public Hearings on Ordinances to Add Pornography as Discrimination Against Women. (1983). Committee on Government Operations, City Council, Minneapolis, MN.

Rachman, S. & Hodgson, R. J. (1968). Experimentally-induced "sexual fetishism": Replication and development. *Psychological Record, 18,* 25-27.

Radford, Jill, and Russell, Diana (Eds.). (1992). *Femicide: The Politics of Woman Killing.* New York: Twayne Publishers.

Russell, Diana. (1975). *The Politics of Rape.* New York: Stein and Day.

Russell, Diana. (1980). Pornography and violence: What does the new research say? In Laura Lederer (Ed.), *Take Back the Night: Women on Pornography* (pp. 218-238). New York: William Morrow.

Russell, Diana. (1984). *Sexual Exploitation: Rape, Child Sexual Abuse, and Workplace Harassment.* Beverly Hills, CA: Sage.

Russell, Diana (Ed.). (1993a). *Making Violence Sexy: Feminist Views on Pornography.* New York: Teachers College Press.

Russell, Diana. (1993b). The experts cop out. In Diana Russell (Ed.), *Making Violence Sexy: Feminist Views on Pornography.* New York: Teachers College Press.

Russell, Diana, and Trocki, Karen. (1985). The impact of pornography on women. Testimony prepared for the Attorney General's Commission on Pornography Hearings, Houston, Texas, 11 September.

Scully, Diana. (1985). The role of violent pornography in justifying rape. Paper prepared for the Attorney General's Commission on Pornography Hearings, Houston, TX.

Senn, Charlene. (1993). The research on women and pornography: The many faces of harm. In Diana Russell (Ed.), *Making Violence Sexy: Feminist Views on Pornography.* New York: Teachers College Press.

Senn, Charlene. (1992, June). Women's contact with male consumers: One link between pornography and women's experiences of male violence. Paper presented at the Canadian Psychological Association Meetings, Quebec.

Senn, Charlene. (1992). Women's responses to pornography. In Diana Russell (Ed.), *Making Violence Sexy: Feminist Views on Pornography.* New York: Teachers College Press.

Senn, Charlene, and Radtke, Lorraine. (1986, June). A comparison of women's reactions to violent pornography, non-violent pornography, and erotica. Paper presented at the Canadian Psychological Association, Toronto.

Silbert, Mimi, and Pines, Ayala. (1984). Pornography and sexual abuse of women. *Sex Roles, 10*(11-12), 857-868.

Smith, Don. (1976). Sexual aggression in American pornography: The stereotype of rape. Paper presented at the American Sociological Association Meetings, New York, NY.

Theodorson, George, and Theodorson, Achilles. (1979). *A Modern Dictionary of Sociology.* New York: Barnes and Noble.

White, Van. (1984, September). Pornography and pride. *Essence.*

Zillmann, Dolf. (1985). Unpublished transcript of testimony to the Attorney General's Commission on Pornography Hearings, Houston, TX, pp. 110-157.

Zillmann, Dolf, and Bryant, Jennings. (1984). Effects of massive exposure to pornography. In Neil Malamuth and Edward Donnerstein (Eds.), *Pornography and Sexual Aggression,* (pp.115-138). New York: Academic Press.

FEMINIST ANTI-PORNOGRAPHY
EDUCATION AND ACTIVIST ORGANIZATIONS

Compiled by Jan Woodcock

This list is undoubtedly incomplete. Please send the names of any other feminist organizations that should be included here to International Networks (see the address below). Hopefully, they can be included in any future printings of this book.

Eastern United States

Women's Alliance Against Pornography, P.O. Box 4, Northampton, Massachusetts 01061-0004

Women's Alliance Against Pornography, P.O. Box 2027, Cambridge, Massachusetts 02238

New York Anti-Sexist Men's Action Network, P.O. Box 150-786, Van Brunt Station, Brooklyn, New York 11215

Women Against Pornography (W.A.P.), P.O. Box 845, Times Square Post Office, New York, New York 10108-0845

Men Against Rape and Pornography, P.O. Box 81856, Pittsburgh, Pennsylvania 15217

Men's Anti-Rape Resource Center, P.O. Box 73559, Washington, DC 20056

Feminists Fighting Pornography, P.O. Box 6731, Yorkville Station, New York, New York 10128

Pornography Awareness, Inc., c/o Southern Sisters Book Store, 411 Morris Street, Durham, North Carolina 27701

Canada & Midwestern United States

Montreal Men Against Sexism, 913 de Bienville, Montreal, Quebec H2J 1V2

Resources Against Pornography (R.A.P.), P.O. Box 695, Toronto Postal Station "C", Toronto, Ontario, Canada M6J 3S1

International Networks, P.O. Box 1068, Mt. Pleasant, Michigan 48804-1068

Women's Resource Center, c/o Dept. of Political Science, 1200 Academy St., Kalamazoo College, Kalamazoo, Michigan 49007

Students Organizing Against Pornography, Dept. of Philosophy, Miami University, Oxford, Ohio 45056

Sexual Violence Center, 1222 W. 31st Street, Minneapolis, Minnesota 55408

Men Stopping Rape, Inc., P.O. Box 316, 306 North Brooks Street, Madison, Wisconsin 53715

W.H.I.S.P.E.R. (Women Hurt In Systems of Prostitution Engage in Revolt), P.O. Box 8719, Lake Street Station, Minneapolis, Minnesota 55408

Northwestern United States

Council For Prostitution Alternatives (C.P.A.), 710 S.E. Grand Ave., Suite 8, Portland, Oregon 97214

Stopping Violence Against Women (S.V.A.W.), c/o Downtown Women's Center, 511 S.W. 10th, Suite 905, Portland, Oregon 97205

Men's Issues Discussion Group, Reed College, 3203 S.E. Woodstock Blvd., Portland, Oregon 97202

Citizens Opposed To Media Exploitation, 926 N. State Street, Bellingham, Washington 98226

Mexico & Southwestern United States

Centro de Orientacion y Apoyo a la Mujer, 6 a. Rayon y Victoria #99, Apdo. Postal 1133, Suc. "A", H. Matamoros, Tam. Mexico

Centro de Orientacion y Apoya a la Mujer, P.O. Box 4282, Brownsville, Texas 78520

Media Watch, P.O. Box 618, Santa Cruz, California 95061

Always Causing Legal Unrest (A.C.L.U.), P.O. Box 2085, Rancho Cordova, California 95741-2085

Naturists and Nudists Opposing Pornographic Exploitation, and Citizens for Media Responsibility, can also be contacted at the A.C.L.U. address.

National Organization For Men Against Sexism, c/o M.O.V.E., 54 Mint Street, Suite 300, San Francisco, California 94103

ABOUT THE AUTHOR

Diana E. H. Russell obtained a Postgraduate Diploma (with Distinction) from the London School of Economics and Political Science in 1961. She was the recipient of LSE's Mostyn Lloyd Memorial Prize awarded to the best student studying for the Postgraduate Diploma. She received her Ph.D. from Harvard University in 1970.

Diana is Professor Emerita of Sociology at Mills College, Oakland, California, where she taught sociology and women's studies for 22 years. She is author or editor of 11 books (see the list at the beginning of the book). *The Secret Trauma* won the 1986 C. Wright Mills Award. This award is given annually by the Society for the Study of Social Problems for outstanding social science research that addresses an important social issue.

Diana has been active in the women's liberation movement since 1969. She started teaching the first course in women's studies at Mills College at that time. She was one of the main organizers of the 1976 International Tribunal on Crimes Against Women. In 1976 Diana became one of the founding members of the first feminist anti-pornography organization in the U.S. (Women Against Violence in Pornography and Media — WAVPM). She remained active in this organization for many years.

Diana has lectured widely, in the United States and abroad, about the political situation in South Africa, rape, incest, child sexual abuse in general, pornography, and all forms of violence against women. She has been arrested three times for her political activism, in South Africa (1963), in England (1974), and in the United States (1990).

Diana is currently conducting interviews with incest survivors in South Africa for a book entitled, *Telling Men's Secrets: South African Incest Survivors Speak Out*. She is also looking for a publisher for a book of case studies of woman-killing titled *Fatal Attractions*. She will be returning to the United States in September 1993.

Cassandra Parker

INDEX